The Very Surprising History of

Fish and Chips

**How refugees, revolution and railways made
The British Classic**

by

Glyn Hughes

Author of 'The Lost Foods of England'

2022

COPYRIGHT INFORMATION

Published for
The Foods of England Project
Denver House
Winster
Derbyshire
England DE4 2DH

www.foodsofengland.co.uk

This print edition ISBN: 978-1-4716-3165-8
(Digital edition ISBN: 978-1-4716-2650-0)

Also by Glyn Hughes:

The Lost Foods of England - the vast great-grandmother of all English cookbooks, more than 1000 receipts for lost and forgotten dishes from Pandewaff to Salmagundi.

The Forme of Cury - The original text from the Master-Cooks of King Richard II, with a new modern English translation and enchanting illustrations from the Lutteral Psalter

CONTENTS

The Very Surprising History of Fish and Chips

TO BEGIN

There is nothing more British than Fish and Chips.

If you put that precise phrase "there is nothing more British than Fish and Chips" into a well-known Internet Search Engine, you get 1,630 documents with *exactly* that phrase. Slightly interestingly, the same phrase, but 'English' instead of 'British', finds just three.

And British it is, isn't it? The Fish and Chip historian John K Walton quotes trade journalist John Stephen back in 1933...

> Have we another food-catering trade so national in character as the fried-fish trade? I doubt it. Fish landed by British ships, manned by British fishermen, searching the seas from close inshore to the Arctic regions, in fair weather and foul; potatoes grown on our home farms, dripping from home cattle, ranges made by British labour in British factories, and the fuel, coal or gas, from British mines.

First, let's be clear, what we're talking about here is British Fish and Chips. Which means a fish steak or slice, about the size of a hand, deep-fried in batter and accompanied by 'chips' (which are not 'crisps') of fried potato batons, about the size of a finger. It does not mean goujons, nuggets or fishcakes. It does not mean straw chips, not potato roundels or game chips or mash. And batter means batter, not crumbs or *tempura*.

So, that's that. *There is nothing more British than Fish and Chips.*

Well, we'll see…

The Very Surprising History of Fish and Chips

COMMON FOOD

People have probably been cooking various types of fish in various types of coatings, and more than likely accompanying them with fried root vegetables of some sort, more-or-less forever. But the origin of 'our' Fish and Chips is remarkably difficult to pin down.

Which is the nature of so much food history – common people's stuff, mostly, doesn't get written down and we have to try to put a history together from gleanings. Fish and chips is common people's food.

Derek Oddy's 'Food, drink and nutrition' in the *Cambridge Social History of Britain*, doesn't mention fish and chips at all. Even Redcliffe Salaman, the British physician, pathologist, botanist and potato breeder in his giant *History And Social Influence Of The Potato* gives Fish and Chips just one tiny footnote on page 234, although he does include a brief discussion of the rise of the potato crisp.

Fish and Chips, you see, isn't, or at least wasn't, really 'respectable'. It's a greasy, smelly thing wrapped in old newspapers, bought out of steamy takeaways, eaten (horror!) with the fingers, or even (horror all horrors!) munched outdoors. Something of low status with which respectable people should not become involved, except perhaps on holiday or if they need to give the impression of being honestly egalitarian.

So unrespectable that under the old Public Health Act of 1875 fish frying could be declared to be an "offensive trade", along with blood boiling and tripe dressing. This was part of a general theory of the time that diseases were caused by the 'miasma' of bad smells. A theory which had been thoroughly de-bunked by Dr John Snow's research into cholera in 1855[i], yet the *Fish Trades Gazette*[ii] in 1914 could report George Driver, Bradford's inspector of fish and chip shops that, "it would be a very serious blow to the fried-fish trade if a death took place which could be traced to typhoid fever contracted through the smells emanating from the cellars of a fish shop". Ever relaxed in catching-up on science, rules requiring the prevention of these (entirely non-existent) miasmatic fumes continued to be part of UK Building Regulations until the 1990s.

It seems difficult, nowadays, to imagine how the delicious smell of Chips or Fish frying could be considered in any way unpleasant, let alone dangerous. But it was. Perhaps the old chip ranges burning raw, bitumen-laden coal were the problem. Or maybe less-than-fresh fat was the cause. But there may be a very much more sinister reason. Here's George Orwell in the 1937 *The Road to Wigan Pier...*

> But there was another and more serious difficulty. Here you come to the real secret of class distinctions in the West.. It is summed up in four frightful words.. The lower classes smell.

> That was what we were taught—the lower classes smell. And here, obviously, you are at an impassable barrier. Race-hatred, religious hatred, differences of education, of temperament, of intellect, even differences of moral code, can be got over; but physical repulsion cannot.

Newspapers and court reports of the 1800s are packed with stories of Chipped Potato vendors and Fried Fish merchants being fined for the smell. It might have been ignored if they kept to their place, but when, in 1891, a mobile 'Chipped Potato Cart' turned up in posh Castle Street in Liverpool, young George Williams and his colleagues found themselves in court accused of creating a "vile and abominable odour". The magistrate, Mr Oulton, asked his legal clerk if there was any law against this, and on being told "No", fined them a total of 7 shillings anyway[iii].

There's a story told, again in John K. Walton's *'History of Fish & Chips & the British Working Class',* of a Doctor's wife in 1932 who paid the grocer's boy a few coppers to fetch the fish from the shop as she waited at the end of the street, as she did not think it would do her husband any good if the public knew he ate fish and chips.

Jeeves may have been able rustle-up a quick Worcester Hollandaise for Bertie Wooster's Eggs Benedict, but he never serves him with Fish and Chips. And when Dorothy L Sayers' Lord Peter Wimsey in *The Unpleasantness at the Bellona Club* in 1921 does go out for a fish and chip supper, he is clearly just being daringly maverick to gain the admiration of a Bohemian sculptress.

Of more than 60,000 older works of literature stored online by the Gutenberg Project, 32 have mention of Fish and Chips. Which is rather surprising, seeing as the word 'caviar' gets 1,210 mentions and 25,800 have the word 'Champagne'. Which tells us something about who writes novels, and nothing at all about how popular different foods are, or were. Here are a few excerpts, and you can judge the mood of the times for yourself..

Back to George Orwell and *The Road to Wigan Pier,* here telling how the poorer sorts subsisted on "mostly slices of bread-and-marg and packets of fish and chips", and...

> It is quite likely that fish and chips, art-silk stockings, tinned salmon, cut-price chocolate (five two-ounce bars for sixpence), the movies, the radio, strong tea and the Football Pools have between them averted revolution.
>
> Therefore we are sometimes told that the whole thing is an astute manoeuvre by the governing class – a sort of "bread and circuses" business – to hold the unemployed down. What I have seen of our governing class does not convince me that they have that much intelligence. The thing has happened, but by an unconscious process – the quite natural interaction between the manufacturer's need for a market and the need of half-starved people for cheap palliatives.

Alfred Ollivant, the Sussex writer and sometime army officer in his 1919 novel *Two Men* tells us how, while the more polished Briton abroad might appreciate the sights and smells of foreign, the less sophisticated only dream of one thing. And they can't not speak proper, neither...

> In the Canal he marked the black hair-tents of the travelling Bedouins, and saw a British Camel Corps trekking slowly across the desert against the hills beyond. He sweated in the Red Sea and gazed with awe at the sultry rocks of Aden, and followed with

delight the flying-fish skimming across the Indian Ocean.

Then one dawn the engines stopped; the ship lay at rest; and in his nostrils, blown from the land, there was the smell of incense.

"Makes you think of the Queen of Sheba," said Ernie. "Spices and Tyre and Sidon and all the rest,"...

"Not alf," said his unimaginative friend. "Give me the Pevensey Road o Sadaday nights. Fried fish and chips."

It has been suggested that Britain's reliance on easily-caught, and never-rationed, seafood and easily-grown potatoes was one of the reasons for Allied success in the 1914-18 War, unlike the silly Germans with their reliance on meat. I suspect that would have been the view of Captain James Belton ('late of the British and Canadian Forces') and his chum Lieutenant EG Odell (24th Canadian Battalion) from the general tone of their memoir of the war titled *Hunting The Hun*...

> I was very much impressed with an old lady who kept a fish and chip shop. Her establishment had been partially destroyed. One-half of the window had been blown out and on the other half of the window was displayed a sign which read "Damn the Zeppelins. To Hell with the Kaiser. Fish and Chips as Usual." This shows the spirit of the women of Britain. You can't beat morale like that.

The Oxford-educated poet Louis Golding might have been all-out against war and all for the lower classes, but, here in lines from his

'Sorrows of War' it seems pretty clear he knows which class of person eats fish and chips…

> Abundant woman panting there,
> Whose breast is flecked with spots of grease
> That splutter from your laboured hair,
> O dew-lapped woman, you who reek
> Of stout and steak and fish and chips,
> Why does the short indignant shriek
> Come toppling from your fleshy lips;
> Because, poor smitten fool, I dare
>
> To breathe the outcast name of Peace?

Regeneration, Rider Haggard's 1910 account of the social work of the salvation army helpfully explains that..

> The poor of this district, she said, 'generally live upon fried fish and chips. You know they cannot cook, anyway they don't, and what they do cook is all done in the frying-pan, which is also a very convenient article to pawn. They don't understand economy, for when they have a bit of money they will buy in food and have a big feast, not thinking of the days when there will be little or nothing. Then, again, they buy their goods in small portions; for instance, their coal by the ha'p'orth or their wood by the farthing's-worth, which, in fact, works out at a great profit to the dealers. Or they buy a farthing's-worth of tea, which is boiled up again and again till it is awful-looking stuff.'

The satirical journal 'Punch', which ran from in the 1841 to 1992, was another true British Institution. It ought to have been packed with hilarious jokes about Fried Fish and Chipped Potatoes. But it isn't. There's just a couple of cartoons, which, presumably, seemed much funnier at the time.

Impudence (to Dignity) "Ye'd better look sharp, my lord, if yer wants to be in time for supper. Why, the tripe-and-onions is all gone, and so's the liver-and-bacon; and blest if they hain't sendin' round the corner for all the fried fish as they can lay 'old on"
(1876)

Actor (who has brought friend in for supper—to lodging-house keeper). "Tut, tut, Ma! Cease your apologies. What if there is but twopennyworth of fish and chips? Bring it forth. This is Bohemia!"
Ma (politely bowing to stranger). "How d'ye do, Sir?" (1920)

This is from *The Hand in the Dark* by Arthur J. Rees (author of *The Shrieking Pit*) in 1920…

> They travelled by 'bus from Grays Inn Road as far as Oxford Circus, and walked along a number of quiet secluded streets—the backwaters of the West End—in order to reach Sherryman Street from the lower end, which, with a true sense of the fitness of things, was called Sherryman Street Approach. If the Approach had not been within a stone's throw of Sherryman Square it might have

been called a slum. It had tenement houses with swarms of squalid children playing in the open doorways, its shops offered East End food—mussels and whelks, "two-eyed steaks," reeking fish-and-chips, and horsemeat for the cheap foreign element. There were several public-houses with groups of women outside drinking and gossiping, all wearing the black shawls which are as emblematic of the lower class London woman as a chasuble to a priest, or a blue tattooed upper lip to a high-caste Maori beauty.

It is quite difficult to know anything about the, very popular in his day, author Thomas Burke as, although he seems to have come from middle-class suburbia, he spent considerable amount of his time and effort fabricating stories that he had great personal knowledge of life among the lower classes, and particularly the immigrant communities, who he wrote about.

This is from *Limehouse Nights*, published in 1919, about the low area of London where Fried Fish is not only food for the inferior orders, but, once again, has a suspicious hint of foreigners, and smell, around it..

..the fried-fish shops that punctuate every corner in the surrounding maze of streets, with their assorted rags,

their broken iron, and their glum-faced basins of kitchen waste; and the lurid-seeming creatures that glide from nowhere into nothing—Arab, Lascar, Pacific Islander, Chinky, Hindoo, and so on, each carrying his own perfume.

The fancy lady encounters a room occupied by an immigrant, which may be tiny and carpet-free but the giveaway that it's really, really low, is the presence of Fish and Chips…

> Lady Dorothy gazed around. She saw a carpetless room, furnished only with a bed on the floor, a couple of chairs, and a table littered with fried fish and chips and a couple of stone jugs. In the elusive twilight, it was impossible to obtain a single full view, and the bobbing candle made this still more difficult. By the table stood Henry, in all his greasy glory, a tasteful set-off to the walls which dripped with moisture from the railway above.
>
> Oh! And again—oh! And did people really live down here? Was it allowed? .. Did they eat and sleep and do everything here? .. Dear-dear. How terrible.

Then again, even if Fish and Chips might not be high-class food, it could possibly have a more spiritual dimension, too. This from *Forward from Babylon* by Louis Golding, 1921…

> The worshipper entered the synagogue through a narrow door to the left of an establishment for fried fish and chips. The odour, therefore, of these commodities rising through the building interpenetrated the atmosphere of prayer, until prayer and chipped potatoes became inextricably woven together, and at no period in his life could Philip pass beyond a fried fish shop without feeling a far-off refluence from the old call to worship. Indeed, Philip's earliest anthropomorphism represented the Deity as some immense

celestial figure in white cloth and a white hat standing above the fume and splendour of a great concave oven where He shovelled upon his tray the souls of human beings, brown and crisp, and resembling mystically the strips of potatoes shovelled by Mr. Marks upon a less divine tray in a chip-shop less august.

PESCADO FRITO A LA JUDIA

Obviously, to trace the history of Fish and Chips, we need to begin at its very beginning. So we'll begin in Jerusalem about one hundred years after the death of Jesus Christ.

In the year 136 Simon Bar-Kokhba led what turned out to be the last of a series of revolts against Roman rule in Palestine. The uprising failed utterly, some 580,000 Jews perished and the Emperor Hadrian, he of The Wall, banned all Jews from their own city, from Jerusalem. They fled and dispersed, and a great many found their way along the Mediterranean coast and into Iberia – into what is now Spain and Portugal.

In 711 the Muslims conquered Iberia. But the new rulers of what was called the Caliphate of al-Andalus took seriously the teachings of the Prophet Mohammed that...

> "Those who believe, and those who follow the Jewish way, the Christians and the Sabians[1], and any who believe in God and the Last Day, and who act with decency, they shall have their reward with the Lord, they need have no fear from us, nor need they worry." *Quran, Sura 2.62*

> and..

> "Let there be no compulsion in religion", "You have your way, and I have my Way." *Quran, Suras 2.256, 109.6*

---

1   The 'Sabians' are a bit of a mystery, they may have been the followers of John the Baptist.

… and for 781 years, apart from being required to pay a slightly higher 'Jizya' welfare tax, the 'Sephardic' Jewish communities were accorded the status of 'Dhimmi', a 'protected group' and prospered and grew alongside their Christian and Muslim fellows in Spain. In fact, this period of sharing and studying each other's ideas is often thought of as a "Golden Age of Jewish scholarship".

Unfortunately, things did not go so well for them after Spain was conquered by Christians in 1492. Within days of defeating the last Muslim kingdom at Granada, Queen Isabella of Castile and King Ferdinand of Aragon issued the 'Alhambra Decree' ordering the expulsion of all practising Jews.

Once again, a whole Jewish community became refugees. The largest number accepted the hospitality of Sultan Bayezid and moved to what is now Turkey or Iraq. Some went to the Netherlands, to Germany or France. And some of the refugees came to Britain.

The Jews had been expelled from England by King Edward I in 1290, though that doesn't seem to have been strictly enforced, there are records of Jews in England in the 1400s and 1500s. The expulsion was effectively rescinded in 1657 during the period when England was, briefly, a king-free Republic.

We know the Sephardim had a synagogue in England the 1600s, we know that Queen Elizabeth I's personal physician was a Sephardic Jew[2], and their Bevis Marks Synagogue in London, founded in 1701, is still active to this day. They brought with them their

---

2   Roderigo Lopes, 1517-94. Queen Elizabeth eventually had him hanged, though that seems to be what she did to quite a lot of her favourites.

Page 149.

The Great Synagogue of Toledo,
from The Jews of Spain and Portugal, by EH Lindo, 1848

traditions of scholarship and singing, and, of course, their traditions of food.

Now, the Jewish rules about food hygiene, such as; don't eat pork or shellfish or owls, are well-known, and probably made a lot of good sense at the time. But that's not what we're concerned about when it comes to Fish and Chips. What matters in the creation of the Great British Dish is the rule forbidding cooking on the sabbath.

You know, by heart, of course, the third Commandment (or possibly the fourth, depending on how you count them), which says...

> Remember the sabbath day, to keep it holy. Six days shalt thou labour, and do all thy work: 20:10 But the seventh day is the sabbath of the LORD thy God: in it thou shalt not do any work, thou, nor thy son, nor thy daughter, thy manservant, nor thy maidservant, nor thy cattle, nor thy stranger that is within thy gates: 20:11 For in six days the LORD made heaven and earth, the sea, and all that in them is, and rested the seventh day: wherefore the LORD blessed the sabbath day, and hallowed it. *Torah, Exodus 20,8*

Which, in an age when far too many people were forced to work far too hard and far too long, a complete day of rest, including even for lower-class people and immigrants, seems a very honourable idea.

No work on the Sabbath. And that, very definitely, means no cooking...

> 16:23 And he said unto them, This is that which the LORD hath said, To morrow is the rest of the holy sabbath unto the LORD: bake that which ye will bake to day, and seethe that ye will seethe; and that which remaineth over lay up for you to be kept until the morning. *Torah, Exodus 16:23*

The Portuguese and Spaniards, even now, eat more fish than any other country in Europe. Britain eats about the European average, 25kg or-so per person per year, the Iberian countries, double that.

But fish goes off quickly in a hot climate. The answer is to briefly fry it in very hot oil, which sterilises the outside and kills the bacteria which would otherwise ruin it. But fish fried like that rapidly dries out and soon becomes tough and unpleasant. So, batter it first, which seals-in the moisture. And there you have *'Pescado frito a la Judia'*, Jewish fried fish, which you can cook on Friday and safely keep overnight (it'll stay warm for a long time with its insulating batter coat) to eat on the Sabbath sure in the knowledge that you're faithfully keeping to the tradition of complete rest on the Holy Day.

It also happens to be very delicious.

More than a thousand years later, in the Victorian Era, the London writer Israel Zangwill could say in his *'Children of the Ghetto'* of..

> "Fried Fried fish, and such fried fish! Only a great poet could sing the praises of the national dish, and the golden age of Hebrew poetry is over."

So, when, and how, did this arrive in England? Odd thing is, old English cookery books are full of receipts[3] for fish and fish dishes, and for this and that in 'battour', but not a sign of battered fish. Here's an example, from the records of the Chief Master-Cook to King Richard II in 1390[iv]. The original reads, "Take Ryghzes and make hem clene and do hem to seeþ, pyke hem clene..." but here's a modern translation...

> Take a ruff-fish and make him clean, and set him to seethe, then pick him clean and fry him in oil. Take almonds and grind them in water or wine and add almonds fried with oil and currants and grind it small with ground garlic and a little salt and strong spices and saffron and boil it well, lay the fish in a vessel and cast the mixture on it and serve it forth.

Which isn't quite the fried fish we're used to now, that doesn't turn up in print until 1747. Everything, I suppose, has to start somewhere.

---

3   The English word is 'receipt'. '*recipe*' is French.

HANNAH GLASSE

The first printed record we've got of how to prepare The Fish comes from Hannah Glasse's *The Art of Cookery, Made Plain and Easy.* It was published in 1747, a year in which England had a German King (George II) France was at war with the Netherlands, Indian troops were fighting the British in Nova Scotia and a Scottish leader was beheaded in London. Which made it a fairly ordinary sort of year for the 18th Century.

Hannah Glasse was quite a character, and how she became 'the first domestic goddess', as Clarissa Dickson Wright called her, is quite a story.

She was born at Greville Street in Hatton Garden in London to Hannah Reynolds, mistress of Isaac Allgood, a prosperous coal-mine owner from Nunwick Hall at Hexham in Northumberland. Isaac was clearly fond of Hannah's, as not only was his illegitimate daughter given the name Hannah, after her mother, Hannah, but his real wife was another Hannah, daughter of 'Isaac of London', a vintner.

After some shenanigans involving Mr Allgood, while drunk, signing over his fortune to his mistress, and his wife tying to get it back, our Hannah took up with an older man, John Glasse, a 30-year-old Irish army officer. On 4 August 1724 the couple were secretly married by special licence, to the general disapproval of the Allgood family.

By 1728 the Glasses were living in New Hall, Broomfield, Essex, and six years later were back to London. Over the coming years

Engraved for Mrs Glasse's Complete art of Cookery.

Hannah gave birth to ten children, five of whom survived, and the family were sufficiently prosperous for her to send her daughters to good local schools and her sons to Eton and Westminster. After a less-than-successful 1845 project trying to sell 'Daffy's Elixir', a patent medicine, Hannah decided to write a cookery book.

The Art of Cookery Made Plain and Easy was printed the following year and sold at "Mrs. Ashburn's China Shop, the corner of Fleet-Ditch", ready-bound for 5 shillings, plain stitched for 3 shillings.

In 1746 Glasse modestly wrote "My book goes on very well and everybody is pleased with it, it is now in the press.. it far exceeds any Thing of the Kind ever yet published". In the introduction she states "I believe I have attempted a Branch of Cookery which Nobody has yet thought worth their while to write upon". This, she explains, is a cookery book for everyone, "If I have not wrote in the high, polite Stile, I hope I shall be forgiven; for my Intention is to instruct the lower Sort, and therefore must treat them in their own Way".

A second edition was published the same year, and some subsequent versions appeared without the author's name, just an anonymous "by a Lady". This led to a strange rumour that the book was written by the botanist John Hill. The famous journalist of the day, Samuel Johnson, wasn't so sure. His biographer, James Boswell, recounts a dinner where the publisher Charles Dilly said that "Mrs. Glasse's Cookery, which is the best, was written by Dr Hill. Half the trade know this." Johnson was doubtful, but sure that it must have been written by a man; "Women can spin very well; but they cannot make a good book of cookery".

The Art of Cookery is a wonderful mixture. Alongside Hannah's own works, about a third of the receipts have been gleaned from earlier texts. Among her originals are the first known curry recipe in English, three recipes for pilau, and an early recipe for ice cream. She was one of the first in England to ever mention vanilla, the first to give a receipt for a jelly trifle, and, remarkably, supplies the first known use the term 'Yorkshire pudding' in print.

She later worked as a dressmaker, acquiring such distinguished clients as Augusta, the Princess of Wales, for whom she appears to have made fancy dress for balls. But she ran up excessive debts, was imprisoned for bankruptcy and eventually forced to sell the copyright of *The Art of Cookery*.

The only record we have of her final years is a notice in the *The Newcastle Courant* of Saturday 8th September 1770 announcing that "Last week died in London, Mrs Glasse, only sister to Sir Lancelot Allgood, of Nunwick, in Northumberland". Where she now rests I have not been able to discover.

We do not really know Hannah Glasses' religious affiliation. We do know she was given Christian baptism as a baby on 24th March 1708 at St Andrews church at Holborn in London. But the proliferation of 'Hannahs' and 'Isaacs' in her family tree does rather suggest a Jewish connection.

Her book has some French, Spanish, Turkish and Italian dishes. And quite a number of Jewish ones, including "To dreſs[4] haddocks the Jews way", and one of the first-known receipts for what we now call 'Lemon Curd', which Mrs Glasse introduces as "Marmalade of Eggs the Jews Way". And, for those who couldn't

---

4   This 'ſ' is the Old English 'long S', used in the middle of words.

face going off Empire-building without a bit of pastrami, "The Jews way to pickle beef which will go good to the Weſt Indies, and keep a year good in the pickle; and with care will go to the Eaſt Indies".

But the one we want to start with is "The Jews Way of preserving Salmon and all Sorts of Fish"

> Original Receipt in *The Art of Cookery, Made Plain and Easy* by Hannah Glasse, 1747

> ### The Jews Way of preserving Salmon, and all Sorts of Fish

> TAKE either salmon, cod, or any large fish, cut off the head, wash it clean, and cut it in slices as crimped cod is, dry it very well in a cloth; then flour it, and dip it in yolks of eggs, and fry it in a great deal of oil, till it is of a fine brown, and well done; take it out, and lay it to drain, till it is very dry and cold.

Which is straightforward enough. Hannah then goes on to explain how this cooked fish will keep for ages. In fact, it can be doused in herbs and spices so that "it can keep good a twelvemonth, and are to be eat cold with oil and vinegar; they will go good to the Eaſt Indies".

Then, in addition to the flour-first-then-egg version, Hannah also gives this version...

> Some love fish in batter; then you must beat an egg fine, and dip your fish in just as you are going to put it in the pan; or as good a batter as any, is a little ale and

flour beat up, just as you are ready for it, and dip the fish, to fry it.

Which is precisely the modern receipt for The Fish, 270-odd years ago.

Let's move on now a mere hundred years, to the great Celebrity Chef of the Victorian era...

ALEXIS SOYER

Alexis Benoît Soyer was born in 1810 at Meaux-en-Brie in France. The region is strongly associated with the Protestant Huguenot community and young Alexis was at first destined for life as an ordained pastor. But he didn't take to the seminary, and became an apprentice at a Paris restaurant.

Just a year after completing his apprenticeship he was head cook at the prestigious Maison Douix restaurant and by 1830 was cook to the Prime Minister, Prince Jules de Polignac.

Unfortunately, this was at a time when, the French Revolution having worked-out less than satisfactorily, the brother of the executed King Louis XVI, namely Charles X, was back on the throne. Which was, in many eyes, even less satisfactory.

On the very day the Second French Revolution broke out, 26th July 1830, armed supporters of the 'Trois Glorieuses' burst into Soyer's Prime-Ministerial kitchen and shot two of his staff. He is said to have escaped a summary execution by breaking into a spirited rendition of the patriotic revolutionary anthem *'La Marseillaise'*, thus ensuring the mob knew he was one of them. Instead of shooting him they carried him shoulder high as a hero.

Soyer, however, decided it was wiser to move, and fled to England. There he joined the household of the Duke of Cambridge, where his brother Philippe was already a cook. He then worked for various other British nobles, and met Harriet Leveson-Gower, the Countess Granville, a well-connected socialite with progressive and charitable leanings, who was to become an important friend and supporter.

In 1837 he married Emma Jones, a popular portrait painter of extraordinary skill. She was, possibly, the youngest person ever to have a painting selected for exhibition at the Royal Academy, having had 'Watercress Woman' selected in 1823 at the age of 10. She had significant social concerns, and one of her finest works is of two African girls reading a book, a painting intended to help promote the anti-slavery movement. Emma died in 1842 following complications suffered in a premature childbirth, said at the time, to have been brought on by a thunderstorm.

A

SHILLING COOKERY

FOR

THE PEOPLE:

EMBRACING

AN ENTIRELY NEW SYSTEM OF PLAIN COOKERY
AND DOMESTIC ECONOMY.

By ALEXIS SOYER,
AUTHOR OF "THE MODERN HOUSEWIFE,"
ETC. ETC.

"Religion feeds the soul, Education the mind, Food the body."
Soyer's Hist-y of F-d.

One Hundred and Tenth Thousand.

LONDON:
GEO. ROUTLEDGE & CO., FARRINGDON STREET.
NEW YORK: 18, BEEKMAN STREET.
1855.
[*The Author of this Work reserves the right of translating it.*]

In 1837 Soyer became head cook at London's Reform Club, at a salary of more than £1,000 a year, about £72,000 in today's money. It was there that he became the first of the modern type of 'celebrity chef'.

He installed a host of newfangled things in the kitchen including gas stoves and refrigeration, and opened them to the public. He gave lectures and presentations, and promoted own-brand products including 'Soyer's Sultana's Sauce', 'Soyer's Perfect Sauce', and a tabletop cooker called 'Soyer's Magic Stove, or, Lilliputian Apparatus'.

During the Irish Famine he supervised soup kitchens. He set up a picture gallery and gave the proceeds to charity. He designed a field stove for the army, devised soldier's rations and began the first army catering corps. British Army catering officers still hold an annual dinner in his honour, at which they use Soyer's old receipts.

SOYER'S MAGIC STOVE.

In 1851, alongside the Great Exhibition, he opened a grand 'Gastronomic Symposium of All Nations' right next door. It was not a financial success, and his site is now the Royal Albert Hall.

And M. Soyer wrote cookery books. He wrote *'Culinary Relaxtion'*, *'Délassements Culinaires'*, *'The Gastronomic Regenerator'*, *'Soyer's Charitable Cookery'*, *'The Poor Man's Regenerator'*, *'The modern Housewife, or ménagère'*, *'The Pantropheon: or, History of Food and Its Preparation from the Earliest Ages of the World'*.

But we're interested here with his gigantically popular *'A Shilling Cookery for The People'* of 1845. This was intended to be a, modestly priced, (one shilling, 1/20 of a pound, about £4.20 in today's money, or so the Bank of England tell me), book to educate and inspire the lower classes on how to make tasty, nutritious, food at modest cost, with simple implements, suited to "the organic mastication of a labouring man."

The book sold more than a million copies (it is still in print today) and includes fascinating instructions on boiled rabbit, potato soup, rice with cod's liver ("if allowed by a medical man"), beef collops, curried tripe, steak toad-in-the-hole. And it includes this...

75. Fried Fish, Jewish Fashion.

This is another excellent way of frying fish, which is constantly is use by the children of Israel, and I cannot recommend it too highly; so much so, that various kinds of fish which many people despise, are excellent cooked by this process; in eating them many persons are deceived, and would suppose them to be the most expensive of fish. The process is at once simple, effective, and economical; not that I would recommend it for invalids, as the process imbibes some of the fat, which, however palatable, would not do for the dyspeptic or invalid.

76. Proceed thus: - Cut one or two pounds of halibut in one piece, lay it in a dish, cover the top with a little salt, put some water in the dish, but not to cover the fish; let it remain thus for one hour. The water being below, causes the salt to penetrate into the fish. Take it out and dry it; cut out the bone, and the fins off; it is then in two pieces. Lay the pieces on the side, and divide them into slices half an inch thick; put into a frying pan, with a quarter of a pound of fat, lard, or dripping (the Jews use oil); then put two ounces of flour into a soup-plate, or basin, which mix with water, to form a smooth batter, not too thick. Dip the fish in it, that the pieces are well covered, then have the fat, not too hot, put the pieces in it, and fry till a nice colour, turning them over. When done, take it out with a slice, let it drain, dish up, and serve. Any kind of sauce that is liked may be used with it; but plain, with a little salt and lemon, is excellent. This fish is often only threepence to fourpence per pound; it containing but little bone renders it very economical. It is excellent cold, and can be eaten with oil, vinegar, and cucumbers, in summer time, and is exceedingly cooling. An egg is an improvement in the batter.

The same fish as before mentioned as fit for frying, may be fried in this manner. Eels are excellent done so; the batter absorbs the oil which is in them.

Flounders may also be done in this way. A little salt should be sprinkled over before serving.

> 77. In some Jewish families all this kind of fish is fried in oil, and dipped in batter, as described above. In some families they dip the fish first in flour, and then in egg, and fry in oil. This plan is superior to that fried in fat or dripping, but more expensive.

This is important, because Soyer was massively influential, and his ideas were directed at ordinary people. It also, once again, gives two possible versions of The Fish, but this time the flour-and-water batter version, the one we know now, is first and very much foremost, and the, probably older and more traditional, flour-and-egg version is relegated to an after-note.

There is a newspaper story[v], which I haven't been able to verify, that; "a biographer of Soyer, the renowned cook, records the almost incredible fact that, after Monsieur had dressed a most recherché dinner, be would run into one of the fried-fish shops of the back slums and devour two pennyworth of coarse fish reeking in hot and rancid dripping or lard. This was his idea of good eating." Sounds about right.

THE FRIED FISH WAREHOUSE

The origin of fried fish is that it keeps well and you can eat it cold. Which led ideally to a trade in itinerant street fried-fish sellers and 'Fried Fish Shops', mostly in and around the Whitechapel area of London, and mostly run by Jewish proprietors. Charles Dickens mentioned a 'fried fish warehouse' in Oliver Twist, published in 1838, where he describes the stomping-ground of Fagin, Bill Sykes and the Artful Dodger...

> Confined as the limits of Field Lane are, it has its barber, its coffee-shop, its beer-shop, and its fried-fish warehouse. It is a commercial colony of itself: the emporium of petty larceny: visited at early morning, and setting-in of dusk, by silent merchants, who traffic in dark back-parlours, and who go as strangely as they come. Here, the clothesman, the shoe-vamper, and the rag-merchant, display their goods, as sign-boards to the petty thief; here, stores of old iron and bones, and heaps of mildewy fragments of woollen-stuff and linen, rust and rot in the grimy cellars.

...and again in *Household Words*...

> GIBBET STREET. Near a shabby market, full of damaged vegetable stuff, hedged in by gin-shops-a narrow, slimy, ill-paved, ill- smelling, worse-looking street, the majority of the houses private but with a sprinkling of marine-stores, rag-shops, chandlers' and fried-fish warehouses, low-browed, doorless door-

ways leading to black rotten staircases, or to tainted backyards.

Henry Mayhew was a journalist who realised that the relatively prosperous readers of his *Morning Chronicle* newspaper lived somewhat isolated lives and knew next-to-nothing about the conditions of ordinary folk. He began a series of articles detailing his interviews and investigations into the lives of London's poor, the costermongers, craftworkers and clerks. These were eventually collected into his vast *London Labour and the London Poor* of 1851, one of the first great sociological studies and an endlessly fascinating read.

Here's his article on the fried fish sellers of London, their daily lives and struggles, their customers and their friendships...

> At the neighbouring races and fairs there is a great sale of fried fish. At last Epsom races, I was told, there were at least fifty purveyors of that dainty from London, half of them perhaps being costermongers, who speculated in it merely for the occasion, preparing it themselves. Three men joined in one speculation, expending 8l. In fish, and did well, selling at the usual profit of cent. Per cent., but with the drawback of considerable expenses. Their customers at the races and fairs are the boys who hold horses or brush clothes, or who sell oranges or nuts, or push at roundabouts, and the costers who are there on business. At Epsom races there was plenty of bread, I was informed, to be picked up on the ground; it had been flung from the carriages after luncheon, and this,

with a piece of fish, supplied a meal or "a relish" to hundreds.

In the public-houses, a slice of bread, 16 or 32 being cut from a quartern loaf—as they are whole or half slices—is sold or offered with the fish for a penny. The cry of the seller is, "fish and bread, a penny." Sometimes for an extra-sized piece, with bread, 2d. Is obtained, but very seldom, and sometimes two pieces are given for 1½d. At the stalls bread is rarely sold with the edible in question.

For the itinerant trade, a neatly painted wooden tray, slung by a leathern strap from the neck, is used: the tray is papered over generally with clean newspapers, and on the paper is spread the shapeless brown lumps of fish. Parsley is often strewn over them, and a salt-box is placed at the discretion of the customer. The trays contain from two to five dozen pieces. I under-stand that no one has a trade greatly in advance of his fellows. The whole body complain of their earnings being far less than was the case four or five years back.

The itinerant fried fish-sellers, when pursuing their avocation, wear generally a jacket of cloth or fustian buttoned round them, but the rest of their attire is hidden by the white sleeves and apron some wear, or by the black calico sleeves and dark woollen aprons worn by others.

THE BAKED POTATO MAN.

" Baked 'taturs!   All 'ot, all 'ot !"

[*From a Daguerreotype by* BEARD.]

Not fried fish, but baked potatoes being sold by a travelling vendor,
from London Labour and the London Poor, 1851

The capital required to start properly in the business is:—frying-pan 2s. (second-hand 9d.); tray 2s. 6d. (second-hand 8d.); salt-box 6d. (second-hand 1d.); and stock-money 5s.—in all 10s. A man has gone into the trade, however, with 1s., which he expended in fish and oil, borrowed a frying-pan, borrowed an old tea-board, and so started on his venture.

Of the Experience of a Fried Fish-seller, and of the Class of Customers.

The man who gave me the following information was well-looking, and might be about 45 or 50. He was poorly dressed, but his old brown surtout fitted him close and well, was jauntily buttoned up to his black satin stock, worn, but of good quality; and, altogether, he had what is understood among a class as "a betterly appearance about him." His statement, as well as those of the other vendors of provisions, is curious in its details of public-house vagaries:—

"I've been in the trade," he said, "seventeen years. Before that, I was a gentleman's servant, and I married a servant-maid, and we had a family, and, on that account, couldn't, either of us, get a situation, though we'd good characters. I was out of employ for seven or eight months, and things was beginning to go to the pawn for a living; but at last, when I gave up any hope of getting into a gentleman's service, I raised 10s., and determined to try something else. I was persuaded, by a friend who kept a beer-shop, to sell oysters at his door. I took his advice, and went to Billingsgate for the first time in my life, and bought a peck of oysters for 2s. 6d. I was dressed respectable then—nothing like the mess and dirt I'm in now" [I may observe, that there was no dirt about him]; "and so the salesman laid it on, but I gave him all he asked. I know a deal better now. I'd never been used to open oysters, and I couldn't do it. I cut my fingers with the knife slipping all over them, and had to hire a man to open for me, or the blood from my cut fingers would have run upon the oysters. For all that, I cleared 2s. 6d. On that peck, and I soon got up to the trade, and did well; till, in two or three months, the season got over, and I was advised, by the same friend, to try fried fish. That suited me. I've lived in good families, where there was first-rate men-cooks, and I know what good cooking means. I bought a dozen plaice; I forget what I gave for them, but they were dearer then than now. For all that, I took between 11s. And 12s. The first night—it was Saturday—that I started; and I stuck to it, and took from 7s. To 10s. Every night, with more, of course, on Saturday, and it was half of it profit then. I cleared a good mechanic's earnings at that time—30s. A week and more. Soon after, I was told that, if agree- able, my wife could have a stall with fried fish, opposite a wine-vaults just opened, and she made nearly half as much as I did on my rounds. I served the public-houses, and soon got known. With some landlords I had the privilege of the parlour, and tap- room, and bar, when other tradesmen have been kept out. The landlords will say to me still: 'You can go in,

Fishy.' Somehow, I got the name of 'Fishy' then, and I've kept it ever since. There was hospitality in those days. I've gone into a room in a public-house, used by mechanics, and one of them has said: 'I'll stand fish round, gentlemen;' and I've supplied fifteen penn'orths. Perhaps he was a stranger, such a sort of customer, that wanted to be agreeable. Now, it's more likely I hear: 'Jack, lend us a penny to buy a bit of fried;' and then Jack says: 'You be d——d! Here, lass, let's have another pint.' The insults and difficulties I've had in the public-house trade is dreadful. I once sold 16d. Worth to three rough-looking fellows I'd never seen before, and they seemed hearty, and asked me to drink with them, so I took a pull; but they wouldn't pay me when I asked, and I waited a goodish bit before I did ask. I thought, at first, it was their fun, but I waited from four to seven, and I found it was no fun. I felt upset, and ran out and told the policeman, but he said it was only a debt, and he couldn't interfere. So I ran to the station, but the head man there said the same, and told me I should hand over the fish with one hand, and hold out the other hand for my money. So I went back to the public-house, and asked for my money—and there was some mechanics that knew me there then—but I got nothing but '—— you's!' and one of 'em used most dreadful language. At last, one of the mechanics said: 'Muzzle him, Fishy, if he won't pay.' He was far bigger than me, him that was one in debt; but my spirit was up, and I let go at him and gave him a bloody nose, and the next hit I knocked him back-

42

wards, I'm sure I don't know how, on to a table; but I fell on him, and he clutched me by the coat-collar—I was respectable dressed then—and half smothered me. He tore the back of my coat, too, and I went home like Jim Crow. The pot-man and the others parted us, and they made the man give me 1s., and the waiter paid me the other 4d., and said he'd take his chance to get it —but he never got it. Another time I went into a bar, and there was a ball in the house, and one of the ball gents came down and gave my basket a kick without ever a word, and started the fish; and in a scuffle—he was a little fellow, but my master—I had this finger put out of joint—you can see that, sir, still—and was in the hospital a week from an injury to my leg; the tiblin bone was hurt, the doctors said" [the tibia.] "I've had my tray kicked over for a lark in a public-house, and a scramble for my fish, and all gone, and no help and no money for me. The landlords always prevent such things, when they can, and interfere for a poor man; but then it's done sudden, and over in an instant. That sort of thing wasn't the worst. I once had some powdery stuff flung sudden over me at a parlour door. My fish fell off, for I jumped, because I felt blinded, and what became of them I don't know; but I aimed at once for home—it was very late—and had to feel my way almost like a blind man. I can't tell what I suffered. I found it was something black, for I kept rubbing my face with my apron, and could just tell it came away black. I let myself in with my latch, and my wife was in bed, and I told her to get up and look

at my face and get some water, and she thought I was
joking, as she was half asleep; but when she got up
and got a light, and a glass, she screamed, and said I
looked such a shiny image; and so I did, as well as I
could see, for it was black lead—such as they use for
grates—that was flung on me. I washed it off, but it
wasn't easy, and my face was sore days after. I had a
respectable coat on then, too, which was greatly
spoiled, and no remedy at all. I don't know who did it
to me. I heard some one say: 'You're served out beau-
tiful.' Its men that calls themselves gentlemen that
does such things. I know the style of them then—it
was eight or ten years ago; they'd heard of Lord ——,
and his goings on. That way it's better now, but worse,
far, in the way of getting a living. I dare say, if I had
dressed in rough corderoys, I shouldn't have been
larked at so much, because they might have thought I
was a regular coster, and a fighter; but I don't like that
sort of thing—I like to be decent and respectable, if I
can.

"I've been in the 'fried' trade ever since, except about
three months that I tried the sandwiches. I didn't do so
well in them, but it was a far easier trade; no carrying
heavy weights all the way from Billingsgate: but I
went back to the fried. Why now, sir, a good week
with me—and I've only myself in the trade now" [he
was a widower]—"is to earn 12s., a poor week is 9s.;
and there's as many of one as of the other. I'm known
to sell the best of fish, and to cook it in the best style. I
think half of us, take it round and round for a year,

44

may earn as much as I do, and the other half about half as much. I think so. I might have saved money, but for a family. I've only one at home with me now, and he really is a good lad. My customers are public-house people that want a relish or a sort of supper with their beer, not so much to drinkers. I sell to tradesmen, too; 4d. Worth for tea or supper. Some of them send to my place, for I'm known. The Great Exhibition can't be any difference to me. I've a regular round. I used to sell a good deal to women of the town, but I don't now. They haven't the money, I believe. Where I took 10s. Of them, eight or ten years ago, I now take only 6d. They may go for other sorts of relishes now; I can't say. The worst of my trade is, that people must have as big penn'orths when fish is dear as when its cheap. I never sold a piece of fish to an Italian boy in my life, though they're Catholics. Indeed, I never saw an Italian boy spend a halfpenny in the streets on anything."

A working-man told me that he often bought fried fish, and accounted it a good to men like himself. He was fond of fried fish to his supper; he couldn't buy half so cheap as the street-sellers, perhaps not a quarter; and, if he could, it would cost him 1d. For dripping to fry the fish in, and he got it ready, and well fried, and generally good, for 1d.

Subsequent inquiries satisfied me that my informant was correct as to his calculations of his fellows' earnings, judging from his own. The price of plaice at

Billingsgate is from ½d. To 2d. Each, according to size (the fried fish purveyors never calculate by the weight), ¾d. Being a fair average. A plaice costing 1d. Will now be fried into four pieces, each 1d.; but the addition of bread, cost of oil, &c., reduces the "fried" peoples' profits to rather less than cent. Per cent. Soles and the other fish are, moreover, 30 per cent. Dearer than plaice. As 150 sellers make as much weekly as my informant, and the other 150 half that amount, we have an average yearly earning of 27l. 6s. In one case, and of 13l. 13s. In the other. Taking only 20l. A year as a medium earning, and adding 90 per cent. For profit, the outlay on the fried fish supplied by London street-sellers is 11,400l.

Fried fish, but served with with bread. So that's the fish. Let us move back in time a bit and see about the chips.

Polly Nathan's fried fish shop in Petticoat Lane. London c1905

THE POTATO ARRIVES

Cooks have been frying small pieces, 'chips', of vegetables in oil since time immemorial, so it is reasonable to assume that the experiment was tried with potatoes not long after they arrived in Europe in the 1500s, though the first actual reference to fried potatoes in an English cookbook is not until Robert May's *'The Accomplisht Cook'* of 1660, and there just in passing as an accompaniment to small birds; "and some artichocks, and potato's boil'd and fried in Butter."

Potatoes originate in South America, famously in Peru, where they've been cultivated as a food for centuries. It seems more than likely that the, mostly Spanish, adventurers and Conquistadores returning to Europe with their booty of silver and gold also brought food for the journey, which probably included potatoes. 'Probably', because, once again, ships stewards are not the sort of lowly people whose work gets much written about.

Christopher Columbus had landed at what is now Venezuela in 1498, but it isn't until 70 years later that we get any record of a potato back in Europe, and that just a receipt for a delivery from the Spanish island of Las Palmas to Antwerp. At the same time it looks likely that it was Spanish fishermen, who used to land fish caught in the Atlantic in Ireland to dry it before the long voyage home, took the potato there.

The first report we have in England of the potato comes from *A briefe and true report of the new found land of Virginia* by Thomas Hariot, published round about 1590...

Openavk are kind of roots of round forme, some of the bignes of walnuts, some far greater, which are found in moist & marish grounds growing many together one by another in ropes, or as thogh they were a string. Being boiled or sodden they are very good meate."

As an employee of Sir Walter Raleigh, it is Hariot who is generally credited with helping to first cultivate the potato in at Raleigh's estates in Ireland, and it was Hariot who took it from there into England. He also happens to have been the first person to make a drawing of the Moon through a telescope, on 26 July 1609, beating the Italian Galileo Galilei by just twelve weeks.

The Potato, from John Gerard's Herbal of 1597

It seems to be the case that early use of potatoes in England, and perhaps the rest of Europe, were the sweet potato, rather than our 'white' or 'Virginia' potato. This may well account for why the French call potatoes *pomme-de-terre*, or 'earth-apples'. From the culinary texts we have it isn't that easy to tell the difference.

The earliest English potato receipts are certainly all for sweet dishes. There's one from Prof. R Bradley in 1728 which includes candied lemons and orange-flower water. Our old friend Hannah Glasse in 1747 adds sugar, wine and currants to a potato pudding and when she does do fried potatoes, they're cut into thin Slices, "as big a Crown-piece... fry them brown, lay them in the Plate or Dish, pour melted Butter, and Sack and Sugar over them". In fact Hanna specifically refers to 'White' potatoes in savoury dishes.

John Gerraard's pioneering Herbal of 1597 says of what we call the Sweet Potato...

> "This Plant (which is called of some Sisarum Peruvianum, or Skirrets of Peru) is generally of us called Potatus, or Potatoes... These roots may serve as a ground or foundation whereon the cunning Confectioner or sugar-baker may work and frame many comfortable delicate conserves, and restorative sweet-meats.

But he says of our 'Virginia Potato'...

> The root is thick, fat, and tuberous, not much differing either in shape, colour, or taste from the common Potatoes, saving that the roots hereof are not so great nor long; some of them are as round as a ball, some oval or egg-fashion; some longer, and others shorter:

the which knobby roots are fastened unto the stalks with an infinite number of thready strings.

Sweet Potato belongs to the bindweed or morning glory family, *Convulvulous* or *Convolvulaceae*. But the White or Virginia Potato – the ordinary potato – is a member of the *Solanaceae* family along with deadly nightshade. One of its early promoters even called it the 'Deadly Nightshade Truffle'. And its leaves and its fruit are indeed poisonous. It seems to be the case that 'white' 'Virginia' potatoes were widely treated as highly suspicious vegetables, fit perhaps for animals, but rarely used for human food. In 1748 France had actually made the cultivation of potatoes illegal, on the grounds that they caused leprosy.

To find out how they came to be universally accepted, we have to move to France, and yet another remarkable character in the history of Fish and Chips.

ANTOINE-AUGUSTIN PARMENTIER

Antoine-Augustin Parmentier was born in 1712 the modest Northern French town of Montdidier, son of a somewhat unsuccessful linen draper. He was apprenticed as a pharmacist.

In 1754 an inexperienced 22 year old British militia officer called George Washington had led an attack on French colonists in Pennsylvania, killing their leader Joseph de Jumonville. Which set off a nasty series of 'French and Indian Wars' between Britain and France over which European Power had the right to control North America.

By 1757 the conflict had spread to Europe itself, Prussia and Spain got involved, George Washington changed his allegiance, and Antoine Parmentier joined the French army as a pharmacist, third-class.

During these 'Seven Years Wars' he was captured and held as a prisoner-of-war in Germany, where they were fed with what the French considered to be mere animal feed – potatoes. With his pharmaceutical training, which at that time was very largely plant-based, he realised that potatoes were entirely edible, nutritious and tasty.

At the beginning of the 1770s France faced a series of bad harvests and the government sought the advice of experts in a search for a more reliable source of food. It was largely due to Parmentier that the Faculty of Medicine in Paris finally declared potatoes to be safe, edible and legal. Parmentier published his *Treatise on the Culture and Use of the Potato* as a solution to food shortages

Antoine-Augustin Parmentier in the costume of a Member of the Academy
Painting by François Dumont, 1812

among the peasantry. Not so much 'let them eat cake', as 'let them eat potatoes'.

Parmentier was appointed to the Paris School of Bakery to help stabilize the national food supply by finding more economical ways of making bread. He published *Manière de faire le pain de pommes de terre, sans mélange de farine*, (The Manner of making potato bread without mixing flour) in which he described how to make potato bread. If you truly want a pure potato-only bread, it gets a bit complicated as it involves separating out the starchy fraction of the potato and drying it. But if you fancy having a go at a more straightforward potato bread, this is his simplest version...

> To prepare good potato bread, use these roots with an equal part of flour of other grains. The potatoes are cooked in water, without the skins, and crushed with a wooden rolling-pin, so that no lumps remain and a smooth, tenacious and viscous paste results. Take half of the ordinary bread flour, with yeast, and the crushed potatoes, mix them together and add the rest of the flour, and such hot water as is necessary. When the dough is sufficiently risen, put it in the oven, observing that the oven is not as hot as usual, and take care to let it cook longer.

Parmentier then began a series of potato publicity stunts, including hosting dinners of potato dishes for such luminaries as the American polymath Benjamin Franklin and the leading chemist Antoine Lavoisier.

He presented bouquets of potato blossoms to the king and queen, and in 1787 King Louis XVI granted him a plot of rather poor quality land near Neuilly, then on the outskirts of Paris, for his botanical experiments. It is said that he had armed guards placed around the potato patch to give the impression of a very valuable crop, only to have the guards removed at night and give peasants the opportunity to steal them. (The same story is told about Frederick the Great in Germany, but, then, there's no reason why they might not both be true.)

It wasn't just potatoes, of course. Parmentier also published on cheese-making, grain storage, wine, mineral water, mushroom-growing, chestnuts, cornbread, and he is considered one of the pioneers of the process for making sugar from beet.

A fascinating range of potato dishes have been named in his honour. The form of small, cubed, potato pieces sautéed in butter called 'Parmentier Potatoes' are pretty well-known, but there's also 'Velouté Parmentier', a potato and leek soup, 'Hachis Parmentier' which is more-or-less shepherd's pie, a salt cod and potato dish and a Parmentier Salad, with potatoes.

M. Parmentier died in 1813 and is buried in the Cimetière du Père-Lachaise in Paris, where his tomb is maintained with a little garden of carefully-tended potatoes and medicinal plants around it.

Parementier on a 12f Stamp

THE STREET FOOD REVOLUTION

Advertisement for the 'Chip Cafe' offering just chips, but with suitable beer or wine for each class. Probably from the Paris Revolt of the 1870s

To find out how potatoes turned into chips, we're staying in France.

In just a couple of generations the population of France had grown from about 20 million in 1700 to some 27 million, making it the most populous state in Europe.

With another 7 million mouths to feed the, essentially medieval, French farming methods could barely cope. Farming was still hugely labour intensive, with little understanding of fertilisers, crop rotation or plant breeding. There were good years and bad, though from 1777 to 1781 there had been warm summers, ample rain, excellent harvests and enough food.

Then, on the 8th June 1783 the Laki fissure split and the Grímsvötn volcano in Iceland erupted, spewing some 40 thousand million tons of dust into the air. A quarter of Iceland's population were dead within weeks. Unusual winds carried the cloud, with its cargo of lung-burning hydrofluoric acid and sulphur, south and east. By the 18th June it reached Berlin and by the 20th it was in Paris. Ships could not leave harbour, trade stopped, and it has been estimated that, in Britain, some 23,000 people died from the fumes.

Volcanic events like this are rare, we only know of about eight in all of human history, but the 'Volcanic Winter' they create can be widespread, long-lasting and alter the climate in strange ways.

Sellers of frites, from The French Painted by Themselves, 1853

The weather became at times unbearably hot, severe thunderstorms led to floods, there was hail that crushed crops and killed cattle, followed by periods of ice that froze-up the water-mills, then drought that dried out almost all of France's grain-growing regions.

By the start of 1789, France was critically short of food. The government had tried hard to stave-off famine, but constant argument between an ineffectual parliament and a profligate king made it difficult to implement any useful policy.

It was against this background that M. Parmentier had been encouraging the take-up of the potato. And with very good reason, potatoes yield about three times as much food energy per growing acre as the wheat France largely relied on, and twenty times as much as beef. The peasantry heard the message and had gratefully started planting potatoes, but it was too late.

It was also against this background that the French government collapsed in May 1789, on 14th July angry citizens stormed the Bastille prison and full-scale revolution broke out.

Food, or the lack of it, was the first cause of the First Revolution, and the potato was its solution. Potatoes therefore became seen as *the* food of Republicans and Revolutionaries.

In 1794 one of those republican revolutionaries, an anonymous author, who we are fairly sure was Catherine Mérigot, published *La Cuisinière Républicaine* (The Republican Cooking-Woman) in which she taught "...the simple way to utilise potatoes, with advice on their preservation". She tells that...

> This first cooking manual of the New Regime is also the first collection of recipes devoted to the potato... The vegetable kingdom offers no plant that provides more health, more convenience, & less expense than Potatoes... We must therefore regard potatoes as one of nature's most precious gifts to humanity.

Her recipes are moderately fancy with plenty of butter, parsley, spring onion, shallots, ingeniously offering maximum revolutionary potatoeyness by having potatoes fried in a batter itself made of mashed potatoes, or potatoes in a potato sauce. But low-class people can't afford fancy add-ons, and they can't afford deep frying, because fats and fuels were expensive. It has to be take-away.

Seller of frites, from The French Painted by Themselves, *1853*

There was already a tradition of Parisian street sellers offering *beignets,* morsels of puffy wheat dough sprinkled with sugar, like little doughnuts, cooked on hot fat over an outdoor charcoal fire and sold in cones of paper. Wheat was in short supply, food was needed, so it was a simple matter to change to cooking patriotic-ally revolutionary fried potatoes.

In his novel *A Tale of Two Cities*, set at this time, Charles Dickens tells of life in the Saint Antoine district of Paris…

> Hunger was the inscription on the baker's shelves, written in every small loaf of his scanty stock of bad bread; at the sausage-shop, in every dead-dog prepara-tion that was offered for sale. Hunger rattled its dry bones among the roasting chestnuts in the turned cylinder; Hunger was shred into atomics in every farthing porringer of husky chips of potato, fried with some reluctant drops of oil.

Are these potato rounds, or the slender lengths of the true chip? Difficult to say. There is an 1831 article in the French food journal *Gastronome*, about the "toothless old crones" at Paris street corners who no longer prepare doughnuts, but have moved-on to fried potatoes...

> First, the earthy rind is scraped away with a serrated knife, revealing a substance which is firm and appet-izing to the eyes, but indigestible and tasteless; these are not doughnuts, the long ones are cut into long lengths, the round ones into rounds, and then, naked and raw they go pell-mell to the bottom of the

blackened pan to be transformed in taste and colour. Frying is a powerful magic.

Then again in *The French Painted by Themselves* (*Les Français peints par eux-mêmes*) of 1853 we hear that, alongside the other assorted street-food sellers…

> … there is another one that is found everywhere, and whose clientele is infinitely more numerous; I mean the seller of fried potatoes. This one is well-established, it has a shop; but what a shop! Sometimes a nook in a doorway, more often than not a little stall, a cane stool, a space just enough to squeeze in the stove, the wood, the pot of oil, the potatoes and the merchant. I must also say that, compared to the sale of black puddings and sausages, the merchant of fried potatoes has progressed; there is something less ragged in his modest costume; his countenance is more agreeable; his voice is less harsh. This is because his clients do not belong only to the unhappy class; the petty bourgeoisie, too, has recourse to his ministry.

So that's France and that's chips. But surely chips are The Belgian National Dish? The distinguished food historian Pierre Leclerc, himself Belgian, defers to their French origin and points to a Bavarian immigrant, Frédéric Krieger, who opened Belgium's first chip shop around 1844, advertising "fried potatoes in the manner of Paris".

HOW CHIPS GOT TO BRITAIN

Successive French revolutions each brought a share of disaffected French cooks to Britain. We've already heard about Alexis Soyer, but there was also the very founder of *Haute Cuisine*, Marie-Antoine Carême who came to cook for the Prince Regent, Louis Eustache Ude who worked for the Earl of Sefton and invented veal custard, Joseph Favre the French-Swiss cook and occasional Italian revolutionary, the great Auguste Escoffier at the London *Ritz*, and no doubt a multitude of less-remembered names, who must surely have brought knowledge of the potato chip with them.

The Potato Eaters, by Vincent van Gogh, 1885

But search as we have through the writings of these upper-class *chefs de cuisine*, which are packed with things to do with potatoes (Escoffier mentions potato 233 times in his grand *Guide to Modern Cookery*) along the lines of gilded croquettes and *veloutés* the, very humble, chip gets not one word.

Then there's Ireland, which had been among the first to take up cultivation of the potato, in a relationship with the tuber which has been both a very happy, and a very unhappy one. Unhappy, of course, because reliance on one crop meant devastation and famine when that one crop failed in the 1840s.

Happy in that we know from census records that the Irish peasantry, fed almost exclusively on potato with just the occasional addition of cabbage, a little pork, some milk and an odd glass of malty stout, while they may not have had much of a comfortable life, seem to have lived longer, and to have been healthier than almost any of their European contemporaries[vi].

In the period we're talking about here, the late 1800s, a generation after the famine years, Connaught, in the West of Ireland, often thought of as one of the poorest places in Europe, actually had by far the lowest death rate and the lowest incidence of diseases like tuberculosis in all the British Isles[vii].

Fit, strong, Irish men provided much, perhaps most, of the muscle which built the railways and cities of the Britain, just as it had been Irish soldiers and officers who had led the field at Waterloo, not the flabby offspring of 'the playing fields of Eton'.

And Irish women? Well, I can't imagine[5] how he found out this gem of information, but listen to what the great Scottish pioneer

---

5   I can imagine.

economist Adam Smith said of people fed on potatoes in the book which is now taken to be the absolute foundation of modern government economics, his 1776 *The Wealth of Nations...*

> ... and those unfortunate women who live by prostitu-
> tion ... the most beautiful women perhaps in the
> British dominions, are said to be, the greater part of
> them, from the lowest rank of people in Ireland, who
> are generally fed with this root.

There is a general assumption, borne out by the 1920's journalist and chip chronicler William 'Chatchip' Loftas, and by a look at trade directories, that potato chips first made their presence in Britain felt in Lancashire. And it is equally generally assumed that this was helped-along by Irish arrivals fleeing the famine in the 1840s or seeking work in the 1890s. Even if their aim was to reach London or Birmingham, Lancashire, with its ports at Liverpool and Fleetwood, was their natural landing-spot for Britain.

There's another, perhaps surprising, reason why Lancashire was, and still is, so welcoming to Irish people with their extra century of potato expertise.

In 1351 Lancaster became a 'Palatinate', a separate 'regality' to the Kingdom of England. The Duke of Lancaster had Sovereign rights, controlled his own courts, appointed his own judges, sher-iffs and civil servants. And, pretty much set his own laws. Which meant they didn't really need to bother too much what the King down in London said. So, despite Henry VIIIs best efforts, Lancashire remained staunchly Roman Catholic, as, uniquely in England, it does to this day, and Irish newcomers, mostly adher-ents of the Old Church, would have found a welcome.

The English courts only got Supreme jurisdiction over Lancaster in 1873, and Lancashire soldiers in the British Army, even now, owe their military allegiance firmly to the Duke of Lancaster[6].

The statistics on the Lancashire chip take-up are simply astonishing. The Ministry of Agriculture found in 1926[viii] that in southern Lancashire, around the manufacturing centres of Manchester and Bolton, more than half of all potato consumption was as chips, while a little farther south in Nottingham or Wales it was only a quarter and in London just one tenth. It was claimed in 1924[ix] that Lancashire fryers consumed three-quarters of all the potatoes grown in the county.

---

6   By luck of inheritance, the Queen of England happens to be the current Duke (Duke, not Duchess) of Lancaster.

BRINGING IT ALL TOGETHER

So that's the fish and the chips. But it doesn't really explain why it took off as a combination so very particularly in Britain. It looks as if there were four factors.

The first was cheap abundant fish. Being an island helps.

The invention of 'trawling', pulling a giant net bag through the sea behind the boat, vastly increased catches. The development first of 'Dogger' boats and then of the fast and hugely influential 'Brixham' trawler gave British fishermen access to the vast stocks of the North Sea. Each boat might carry six tons of fish and the two or three tons of the salt needed to preserve the catch during the long trip home.

Then the introduction of steam-powered fishing vessels, the world's first was built by David Allan in Leith in 1875, meant that, for the first time, cod and other deep-water fish could be brought to shore quickly enough not to need salting.

By the end of the 1800s there were some 3,000 trawlers operating out of Britain, 20,000 fishermen working the North Sea and Grimsby could claim to be the 'largest fishing port in the world'.

But fresh fish needs moving fast, so the second factor was the development of high-speed transport. Which means railways.

British engineers had famously led the development of railways. Other countries weren't far behind, but while Marc Seguin's French railways grew from the centre, British railway development, being an island, was to the coasts, and brought fish.

Then, thirdly, there's the need to keep fish fresh and cool.

It is, just, possible in Britain to store ice from the winter all through to summer, and there are more than a few insulated 'ice houses' still to be seen in the grounds of grand mansions. There had been some attempts to commercially gather and store ice, but it is, obviously, a rather tricky and uncertain business.

In the 1840s the Wenham Lake Ice Company set up harvesting winter ice from a freshwater lake in Massachusetts, storing it, and transporting it across the Atlantic "for the preservation of meat, fish &c for any length of time". By 1844 they had storage depots in London and Liverpool and a sales office on the Strand.

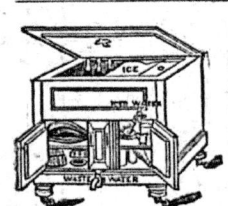

ICE SAFE AND ICE MACHINES.

THE NEW DUPLEX REFRIGERATOR, Registered; for Wenham Lake or Rough I e. Prize Medal Refrigerators, fitted with Water Tan s and Filter. The New American Double Wall Ice Water Pitcher, suitable for Wine Can, &c. The American butter Dish, with revolving lid, for use with ice. Wenham Lake Ice forwarded into the Country in packages of 2s 6d., 4s., 8s., and upwards, by "Goods Train," without perceptible waste.

ICE or ICE CREAMS made in three minutes by the PATENT ICE MAKING MACHINE, with the Improved Freezing Powders. One pint size sufficient for eight persons, £1 2s. 0d. Thirteen kinds of pure syrups supplied for use with the above, for Ices, or for making refreshing Summer Drinks with Aerated Waters, 2s. 6d. per bottle. Clear Ice can be made in this Machine in five minutes. EXHIBITED IN OPERATION DAILY.

Illustrated Price Lists Free on Application.
Wenham Lake Ice Company, 125, Strand, London, W.C.
(Corner of Savoy Street).

Florence Nightingale wrote approvingly of how Wenham Lake ice stopped the milk curdling in summer, Mrs Beeton provided a recipe for a Pineapple Julep using Wenham ice and Queen Victoria granted them her Royal Warrant.

The ice-trade might well have evaporated like its product with the appearance of refrigerators, but early freezers, like the coal-fired one developed in France by Ferdinand Carré and Charles Tellier, were extremely complex and frequently leaked toxic ammonia into the ice. They were also very expensive to run, so warehouse-stored ice harvested from American lakes, or from Norwegian glaciers, remained competitive in price in Britain, and could claim greater purity, into the 1860s.

William Cullen, a Scottish professor of medicine, had demonstrated a simple refrigerator back in 1755 and James Harrison had produced a pioneering commercial version in Australia in 1856.

Not surprisingly, one of the most active markets for ice was in the heat of India, and there large-scale mechanical ice production really took off. Indian merchant had long been importing ice from the Himalayas, and had some success in manufacturing ice in small quantities by a chemical process. Then, taking advantage of the new technologies, in 1886, Subramania Pillai, of the famous spice merchants firm of P. Vencatachellum[7], began the 'South India Ice Factory' at Chenni, then known as Madras. Within two years it was manufacturing some 10,000 lbs of ice a day, and other, even larger, Indian ice enterprises followed.

From the early 1900s, following-on from the German Carl von Linde's and the Dutch Heike Kamerlingh Onnes' discovery of the theory behind cooling (for which Onnes got a Nobel Prize), large-scale freezing became practical and factory-made ice was available to businesses. Which included freezers on-board fishing vessels, allowing deep-sea fish from far-away waters around Iceland and Greenland to be reliably brought to Britain. Only in the 1920s did it became possible and practical to have a refrigerator at home, or in your fish-shop, partly because that required a supply of gas or electricity.

Just in passing, the one invention, rather than a discovery or an observation, made by Albert Einstein was a type of fridge. However, unlike his Theory of Relativity, the Einstein refrigerator doesn't work[x].

---

7   The 'Vencat' brand of 'British' Madras Curry Powder is still going strong.

So that's cheap deep-sea fish, fast transport and freezing. But there's a fourth thing... newspaper.

Newspaper is such an iconic part of the British Fish and Chip experience that, even since it was decided that putting food into inky and well-thumbed waste paper is not a particularly good idea, fake 'newsprint' still adorns chip packaging and chip adverts.

From the appearance of Berrow's Worcester Journal in 1690 (still, being published today, more than 300 years later) governments have tried to censor the news and to control newspapers. Britain tried to tax it.

From 1712 newspapers were subjected to a 'Stamp Tax' on journals that contained any "public news, intelligence or occur-rences, or any remarks or observations thereon, or upon any matter in Church or State." Publishers were required to deposit a bond of £300 (£40,000 in today's money) and pay 4d (£0.60p today) on every copy sold. This was intended to raise money, but also to restrict publications which might "excite hatred and contempt of the Government and holy religion". It successfully damaged the circulation of cheaper papers, which conveniently prevented the lower classes from getting access to up-to-date information or radical news, while having little effect on the wealthy readers.

The tax was increased in 1797, reduced to just one penny 1836 and was finally abolished in 1855, making cheap news available to everyone.

By the 1850s the circulation of English newspapers reached some 122 million copies per week[xi], roughly a paper per person each workday. Which, once they had been read, is an extraordinary amount of waste paper.

Newsprint is a paper manufactured from softwood pulp by a process invented in 1844 by the Canadian poet Charles Fenerty. First produced at the Acadia Paper Mill in Nova Scotia, it is brittle, tears easily and soon discolours under sunlight, but it is also very, very cheap and extremely absorbent. Which is useful for taking-up printing ink very quickly, so high-speed presses could be used. It equally absorbs fats while being sufficiently open in texture to release the steam which makes chips go soggy, making it an ideal Fish and Chip wrapper. Apart, that is, from the poisonous ink leaking off onto your chips together with whatever was on the last reader's fingers.

As early as 1904 the *Fish Trades Gazette* was encouraging the use of greaseproof paper on health grounds, or at least suggesting buying clean newsprint straight from the printers.

It is within our time that you could take waste newspaper to the Chip Shop and get a reward of some scratchings and pea-wet at the stingier shops, or a portion of chips at the more generous ones. There are now plastic trays and card cartons and even bamboo-wood boxes, but it isn't the same, is it?

THE FIRST FISH AND CHIP SHOP

There are several contenders for the prize of having brought The Fish and The Chips together.

One of the contenders is Joseph Malin, born Joseph Malinsky in about 1826, about whom we know little, other than that he was Jewish and owned a fried-fish shop at 78 Cleveland Way, Bow, in East London offering 'fish fried in the Jewish fashion'. At some point in the early 1860s he started selling chips with his fish.

Another possible first was Mr Lees of Mossely, near Oldham in Lancashire, who is said to have sold potato chips from a wooden market kiosk and, around 1863, transferred to a permanent shop which was advertised as a 'chip potato restaurant', with fish.

The interesting thing you'll have noticed is that (London Jewish) Mr Malin had a Fried Fish Shop, which started selling chips, while (Lancastrian) Mr Lees had a Chip Potato Restaurant, which started selling fish.

This makes sense. Lancashire, with its acres of peaty farmland, and a welcome for potato-skilled Irish immigrants led with the potato, and Oldham is little more than a brisk walk away from Manchester's huge Jewish community around Heaton Park and Prestwich, who, we may presume, had long held to the the memory and the practice of fried fish.

London, is sort-of the other-way-round. A long-standing Jewish community where French cooks and Irish peasant refugees were

Great Brunswick Street, Dublin.

welcomed in the 1850s with their potato and frying expertise.

With its much longer history of using potatoes and an island seafaring tradition, Ireland, perhaps ought to have had Fish and Chips before that.

There was a long-established firm of Italian grocers in Dublin begun by Giuseppe Cervi, which was operating at least into the 1990s. Interviewed by the *Evening Herald* in 1976 Tony Cervi, a son of the founder, related how, round about 1882, his father had mistakenly stepped off his America-bound ship in County Cork and walked all the way to Dublin, where he worked as a labourer before saving enough money to buy a cooker and a hand-cart, from which he sold chips, later with fish, outside pubs.

Whether or not Signor Cervi was Ireland's first Fish and Chip seller is not entirely certain, there's also a record of a 'Fried Potato Shop' in Newry in 1869[xii]. But it is certainly the case that there was a wave of immigration, particularly from the comune of Casalattico in Frosinone province, near Rome, at the turn of the 20th century and that Italian families like the Borzas, Fortes, Cafollas and the Macaris dominate the Dublin trade even now.

Tracking-down modest establishments like Fish and Chip shops can be problematical. In the days before Yellow Pages or Google Maps we have to largely depend on the trade directories published for individual towns. But those depended in turn on business-owners being willing to pay for an entry, and if you've got only a small concern and modest income and you're doing fine anyway, then why should you bother?

In Scotland, Dundee lays claim to having offered the first Fish and Chip Suppers in Scotland in the 1870s, sold by a Belgian immigrant in the city's Greenmarket area. Though, as often, the only print record we can find is of a business being put up for sale, and one Edward Degernier did indeed offer his 'Fried Fish and Chip Potato Business' for sale in Dundee in 1891[xiii]. (Someone called Edward Degernier also turns up in court records in Dundee for committing assault in 1882[xiv] and again in 1885, but that may, of course, be a completely different Edward Degernier of Dundee)

In Wales, we find the distinctive phrase 'London fried fish and chipped potato' or 'London chip potatoes' being used by several establishments, including Taylor and Luxmore's restaurant at 147, High Street in Swansea from the 1880s[xv] and a very interesting advertisement from 1887 for a "Dogcart (handsome) for frying London chip potatoes in the street[xvi]".

Even the 'Fish and Chip' name hasn't always been quite what it is now.

We've not been able to track down the precise phrase 'fish and chip' to before, once again, an advertisement offering for sale the "best fried fish and chip potato shop in Manchester" in 1879, suggesting that, by then there were plenty of them. There's a sports-page report of a highly successful rabbit-coursing dog called 'Fish and Chips' in the *Newcastle Daily Chronicle* in 1891[xvii]. But the phrase throughout the Victorian era seems to have usually been variants of 'Fish and Chipped Potato'. The first time we've found the modern usage in print comes from an edition of *Tales and Sketches of Old and New Bristol* by Fred Ludlow, published in 1890, where it is clear that we're not talking about fancy folks' food...

> "I don't know nothin' about that 'ere sort o' grub," replied the astonished Bill Blower, "but I could jest do a feed of fried fish and chips, follered. By a pot of foamin' old and bitter. That's more my mark."

BIG BUSINESS

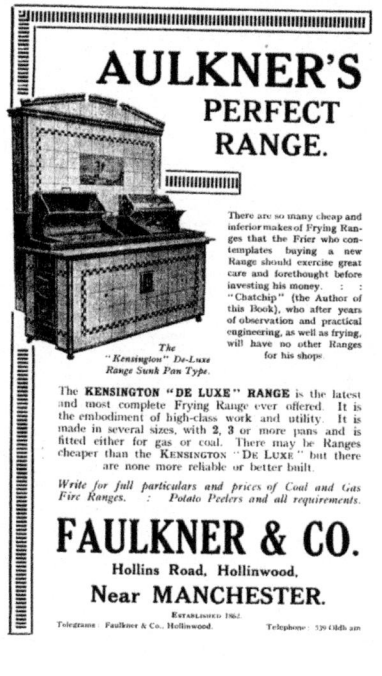

The National Federation of Fish Fryers tell us that...

By 1910 there were perhaps 25,000 fish and chip shops around the country, peaking at 35,000 by 1927 and between the wars most industrial towns boasted a fish and chip shop on almost every street. Fish fryers' consumption on the eve of the First World War was calculated at between 100,000 and 150,000 tons per year. and *Fish Trades Gazette* asserted that: "the estimated number of fryers in the United Kingdom is no fewer than 10,321".

Britain now has about 10,500 chip shops and consumes nearly 400 Million portions of Fish and Chips each year, equal to about six for every man, woman and child. And that's not including fish and chips bought from restaurants, pubs and vans. McDonalds has only 1,200 outlets, Kentucky Fried Chicken just 840.

Since the end of the Second World War, the food landscape in Great Britain has changed in many ways and although its unlikely the number of fish and chip shops will ever again reach the levels of 1920's and 30's the demand for the dish has remained the same.

Today some 10,500 businesses provide the Nation with a similar volume of fish and chips to those of the post war years.

In the 21st Century, many businesses are family owned independents, some 2nd and 3rd generation and are the focal point of many communities. Collectively these businesses use 10% of the UK's potato crop and 30% of all white fish sold in the UK and the industry generates a turnover of around £1.2 billion every year. A total of 62% of fish sold in fish and chip shops is cod and 25% is haddock. 90% of shops use FAS fillets - these fish are caught by large modern trawlers operating in carefully managed fishing grounds in the icy, clear Arctic waters of the Barents Sea and North Atlantic, caught by Icelandic, Norwegian, Russian and Faroese vessels. Stringent, science-based and strictly enforced regulations have ensured good management of cod and haddock stocks in these waters, and the catches from this area accounts for 97% of the total Northern Hemisphere cod quota.

Local fish frying associations had begun cropping up around the country towards the end of the 19th century, providing solidarity for fryers as the industry grew. But it wasn't until the 11th November 1913 that something bigger was realised. Manchester was where it all began, or to be precise the Albion hotel where delegates from 17 local fish frying organisations gathered with the intention to create a singular national body capable of protecting the interests of the trade.

That meeting, called by the Manchester, Salford and District Fish Fryers Association was to form the National Federation of Fish Fryers Associations. The first secretary was William Loftas and the membership fee was one shilling per year.

THE MAN IN OUR FRIED FISH SHOP SAYS:

"Just watch your kids tuck into fish and chips...

... and they'll thrive on it too! You see, fish and chips is a proper meal; good, hot, filling stuff that kids need while they're growing. A jolly sight better for them than these bits of snacks!

" I'm not the only one who says so, either! Some of the most famous doctors in the land'll tell you that fish and chips is the sort of food kids need to feed them properly.

" Another thing ... there aren't a lot of foods that haven't been messed about with chemicals and things nowadays. But my fish is always nice, and fresh and wholesome. And the way I fry it, the kids love it, bless 'em ! "

... and the Whispering Fish says:

If you have kiddies at home, read " Fish for Growing Children". It's free at your fried fish shop, or you can write to me, Whispering Fish, Brettenham House, Lancaster Place, London, W.C.2, and I'll send you one.

ISSUED BY THE WHITE FISH AUTHORITY

Throughout the early part of the 20th century growth of the NFFF was up and down and in no doubt affected by the two world wars, but early champions such as General Secretary Jackson Tomlinson MBE and twice President Henry Youngman cemented the existence and requirement of a fish frying trade body with membership peaking at 10,914 in 1947.

The early years of the NFFF were marred by rivalry within the trade and several breakaway organisations may have put an end to one national body representing fish fryers In 1923 the Northern Counties Federation came into existence drawing members away from the NFFF only for the breakaway body to become re-united a year later. Several years later in 1968 a similar situation arose when the London and Home Counties Association broke away, again, to re-join later in 1991.

Some interesting facts about fish and chips...

A staggering annual spend of £1.2 billion on fish and chips in the UK.

Once a year, at least 80% people visit a fish and chip shop, 22% of people visit fish and chip shops every week. 56% of people buy fish and chips to eat in the home as a family meal.

Fish and chips provide a third of the recommended daily allowance of vitamins for a man and nearly half for a woman.

THE MAN IN OUR FRIED FISH SHOP SAYS...

Mothers with children, and housework to do
Appreciate time-saving tips.
So when you go shopping, remember that you
Can save work with FRIED FISH AND CHIPS.

And the Whispering Fish says:
"SEE THE MAN IN YOUR FRIED FISH SHOP
... he's a dab-hand at frying".

THE WORLD'S ISLAND

So, we have a Jewish recipe from Muslim Iberia for, now largely Icelandic, fish served with a South American vegetable cooked in a French Revolutionary fashion.

I could add to that "and served by a Russian method", because the idea of the diner being presented with a ready-put-together thing-and-two-veg is 'Russian Service', which long ago supplanted the old-fashioned 'English service' where each was given an empty plate to choose what they want.

It is the interplay of ideas and the meeting of people that make things. Fish and Chips was caused by George Washington, King Louis XIV, Napoleon, Mohammed and several Hannahs. And it was invented, too, by a multitude of unnamed heroes, the Jewish immigrant street sellers, Irish fleeing famine and French seeking asylum from revolution, and by whoever it was who first fried her *battonets* of potato by the Pont Neuf. Fish and Chips was made possible because of Carl von Linde's theories, Auguste Parmentier's prison cook and Charles Fenerty's newsprint.

How British is all that?

Well, it is actually the most British thing there could ever be.

Because, by lucky happenchance of geography, Britain just happens to be in just the right place to be *The World's Island* – the place where all the peoples of the world meet together, to bring their oh-so-different ideas. Bringing people together is what Britain does.

Penicillin? Discovered in France by Jules Francois Joubert. But it was in Britain that Alexander Fleming used a technique created in Ireland by Joseph Bigger, CR Boland and RAQ O'Meara to show it was an antibiotic, so that an Australian, Howard Florey, a German, Ernst Chain, an American, Andrew Moyer, could make it into a medicine.

Television? Invented back in 1885 by a German, Paul Nipkow. Georges Rignoux and Alain Fournier had built crude version in Paris in 1909, but it took Britain, and a Scot, John Logie Baird, to put it together with the electronics pioneered by a Bulgarian, Porfiry Bakhmetiev, and a Hungarian, Philipp Lenard, to actually make a sort-of-working TV.

And so on. And on. I mean, even Winston Churchill was the child of an immigrant. In his case it was his mother, but whether it goes back one generation or a multitude, every single one of us in Britain is either an immigrant, or the child of immigrants, and every Great Thing that Britain has ever done has been because we've brought people together.

There is a taste of the world and of *The World's Island* in every bite of Fish and Chips.

(Oh, and the first fish-and-chip shop was some fifty years *after* the first Indian Take-Away in England[8].)

---

8   Opened in 1810 by the extraordinary Bengali businessman Sake Din Mahomet at George Street in London, offering Ladies and Gentlemen "India Dinners, sent to their own houses".

ANYTHING ELSE WITH THAT?

There are strict limitations to what is allowed with Fish and Chips. And some things are not allowed. For the sake of common decency I've had to pixelate-out the little portion of salad on that photo, because salad is clearly a no-no. In fact, if not actually illegal, it ought to be.

But it is worth mentioning a few of the more everyday (and legal) accompaniments and things found on the counter next to the Fish and Chips, each with its own fascinating little story...

Pea-Wet

The reduced water in which dried peas have been boiled, used as a soup or gravy.

Although now rarely met with other than an occasional splashed-on Chip-Shop addition to Fish and Chips, various 19th Century sources (including the Reports of the 1843 *Commissioners on the*

Employment of Children) refer to Pea-Wet as being, with bread, a fairly commonplace breakfast for the lower orders.

Curry Sauce

Although modern curry-lovers might disdain the chip shop style of curry sauce, it is actually more-or-less identical to the receipt developed by the great French *chef de cuisine* Auguste Escoffier ('Cook to Emperors, and Emperor of cooks') during his time at the London Ritz and published in his *'Modern Cookery'* of 1903. Here's the original receipt…

81 CURRY SAUCE

Slightly brown the following vegetables in butter: Twelve oz. of minced onions, one oz. of parsley roots, four oz. of minced celery, a small sprig of thyme, a bit of bay, and a little mace. Sprinkle with two oz. of flour and a teaspoonful of curry pepper.

Cook the flour for some minutes without letting it acquire any colour, and dilute with one and one-half pints of white stock. Boil, cook gently for three-quarters of an hour, and rub through a tammy. Now heat the sauce, remove its grease, and keep it in the bain-marie. Serve this sauce with fish, shell-fish, poultry, and various egg-preparations.

N.B. This sauce is sometimes flavoured with cocoa-nut milk in the proportion of one-quarter of the diluent.

M. Escoffier also produced a recipe for fish and chips, which, in true Escoffier style, is so preposterously posh (Dover sole, chips cut into little balls) that it need have no place in this book.

Savoury Patties

A savoury patty is made from battered and deep fried mashed potato, seasoned with herbs such as sage. It is particularly associated with chip shops in the port towns of Hartlepool, Kingston upon Hull, The Wirral, Liverpool, North Tyneside, Kirkwall and Thurso, though has been encountered in inland Lincolnshire.

Variations include the addition of corned beef, cheese and cheese-and-onion.

At one time patties were prepared on an industrial scale in Yorkshire, largely by women in iconic 'white coats and white wellies, known as the 'Pattie Slappers', with a reputation of forthright sturdiness. A study into their lives called *Pattie Slappers: Stories from the Golden Age of Hull's Food Processing Industry* was published by Nick Triplow, 2013[xviii].

Fishcakes and Fish Scones

A fishcake, a round pattie of minced fish, usually with potato in a crumb coating, can just be a fishcake, of course, but in in parts of the North a 'fishcake' is a disc of minced fish sandwiched by two large slices of whole potato and covered in batter. In parts of Yorkshire these are 'fish scones'.

Mushy Peas

Dried marrowfat peas, reconstituted and boiled with plain water until fallen to a soft mush. Sodium carbonate is sometimes added to the water used to reconstitute the peas so as to prevent chloro-phyll breaking down and preserve a bright green colour.

Although peas cooked until fallen is certainly an ancient dish, we've records of it back to the 1300s, and the word 'mushy' goes back centuries, there doesn't seem to be any *written* record of the actual phrase 'mushy peas' before the TV series *'Last of The Summer Wine'* in 1973 with the line written by Roy Clarke; "Clegg: We only left him last night. Stuffing his face with fish, chips and mushy peas."

('Marrowfat' simply means a mature pea, plump and suitable for drying, and is not in any way connected with the Japanese 'Maro' pea.)

Deep-Fried Mars Bar

Putting a chocolate-caramel Mars Bar in batter and deep-frying it seems so curious an idea that it has often been assumed to be a mere Scots myth along with Nessie and Brig O'Doon. Not so.

It is certainly Scottish in origin, and is claimed to have been invented in 1992 by John Davie in The Haven Chip Bar (now called The Carron) at Stonehaven, near Aberdeen, though there are other claimants including the Duncan Street Chip Shop in Banff and Dodie's Chip Shop in Buckie.

The dish achieved international fame after being featured in Jay Leno's popular 'Tonight' TV show in the USA in 2004, following which the *Lancet* medical journal, with a suspicion that deep fried Mars Bar might not be an entirely healthful food, commissioned the University of Dundee to investigate.[xix].

In their report titled *Deep and crisp and eaten: Scotland's deep-fried Mars bar,* David S Morrison & Mark Petticrew found that...

- 22% of shops responding sold DFMb; three-quarters of those had only been selling them for the past 3 years.
- An additional 17% had sold them in the past.
- Average sales were 23 bars per week, although 10 shops reported selling 50—200 per week.
- The mean price was £0.60 (range £0.30 to £1.50).
- 76% were sold to children.
- 15 shops reported health concerns with the food.

In 2012, the Carron Fish Bar estimated they were selling 100–150 deep-fried Mars bars per week, 70% to visitors who had heard of its reputation.

In 2000 the deep-fried Mars bar reached *Haute Cuisine* at the tables of the Paris *Le Chipper* restaurant (listed in the French restaurant guide 'Les Restos' as "Cuisine type: other") when Scottish chef Ross Kendall included included a fancy version on the menu. Nigella Lawson has tried a deep-fried Bounty bar on her TV show.

In the survey Dr Morrison noted that, "The most frequent comment made to us about the snack was that deep-frying Mars bars spoils the fat or frying equipment. 15 shops reported health concerns. Other interesting foods that the fish and chip shops have been asked to fry include chocolate (21%) and sweets (16%) in general, Snickers (4%), Creme eggs (4%), and pizza (4%). Three shops each said they had been asked for deep-fried ice cream and deep-fried Maltesers. Deep-fried Toffee Crisps, bananas, pineapple rings, and Rolos had also been requested."

The deep-fried Mars bar has been cited as 'all that is wrong with the high-fat, high-sugar Scottish diet' and has led to number of further academic studies including the splendidly-titled *A randomised crossover trial of the acute effects of a deep-fried Mars bar or porridge on the cerebral vasculature* of 2014[xx]

The Lancet study concluded that, "Scotland's deep-fried Mars bar is not just an urban myth. Encouragingly, we did also find some evidence of the penetrance of the Mediterranean diet into Scotland, albeit in the form of deep-fried pizza."

Non-Brewed Condiment

When you ask for vinegar in your local chippy, a sober sideways glance at the bottle may reveal that it doesn't say 'vinegar' on it but instead the rather-suspicious-sounding 'Non-Brewed Condiment'. Which could be, perhaps, some sort of cheap vinegar substitute? Unlikely, as vinegar is already just about the cheapest product[9] there is on any supermarket shelf.

Non-Brewed Condiment is in fact essentially exactly the same substance as vinegar, but produced by a different process which doesn't involve any brewing. Traditional vinegar, of course, is made by treating beer with acetobacter bacteria which converts the alcohol into sharp-tasting acetic acid. The Non-Brewed version seems to have its origins with the beer-disdaining Temperance Movement of the early 20th Century. The movement's other great non-brewed achievements like Aerated Bread and Botanical Beer have more-or-less disappeared, but the Condiment has stayed with us, largely, I think, because the N-B-C process can make a stronger

---

9   Vinegar at Aldi (2022) works out at £0.01p per litre more expensive than their cheapest water. But water isn't really a 'product' is it?

stuff, which uses less packaging and transport and can then be diluted as you fancy. The leading providers are Drywhite Ltd, whose concentrated form of Non-Brewed-Condiment is called 'Maltflaven'.

Tartare Sauce

Mayonnaise with chopped capers, gherkin and vinegar.

Tartare was formerly made with other sharply-flavoured ingredients. Eliza Acton in 1845 makes it with mustard, shallots and parsley as well as the capers and gherkins while another version uses tarragon vinegar.

Scratchings

Stray portions of batter from frying fish, sold, or given away, separately, in chip shops. More common in the North, and sometimes enlivened with Pea-Wet for those who cannot find the money for a more substantial meal. They are known by this name at least since 1904[xxi] and as an item of trade for recycling at least since an advertisement in Liverpool in 1914[xxii] "Wanted - CHIP Shop Scratchings and Old Fat"

This is similar to the ancient forms of fried batter known as 'Cryspels'. There is also a similar tradition of 'Tenkasu' in Japan, from stray bits of the tempura batter used in Japanese cuisine.

Scallops

While many chip shops may indeed serve other seafood, such as actual scallops, in Northern chip-shop practice, these are now large rounds of potato, cut about 3/8ins thick, battered and deep-fried.

Orange Chips

A West Midlands chip-shop speciality, a style of potato chip dipped in an orange coloured batter, sometimes with paprika, before being fried. They are a relatively recent innovation, and we have an original receipt…

Original Receipt from Birmingham Mail, 2 May 2020
To make orange chips from home you will need:
A deep fat fryer
Your cooking oil of choice
Four large potatoes
½ tsp salt
½ tsp black pepper
½ tsp garlic powder
½ tsp paprika
1 cup plain flour
1 tsp baking powder
½ cup milk
½ cup water
Orange food colouring

What do you do? Firstly chop peel and wash your potatoes then chop them up to form the chips.
Next, make your batter. Combine the dry ingredients above in a mixing bowl. Slowly add the wet ingredients making sure you whisk as you pour to form a smooth mixture. Add a few drops of the orange food colouring. Then coat your chopped potatoes in flour then dip them in the batter mixture.

The Spice Bag

A spice bag is a distinctive method of serving chips in Irish, particularly, Dublin, Fish and Chip shops, where a bag of chips, often with chicken, is topped with a mixture of sautéed vegetables such as peppers with spices. The origin is unknown, but very recent.

Jamaican Patties

These are type of pasty, a folded-over pastry filled with spiced meat and vegetables which have become a very regular feature of Birmingham Chip Shops.

They can fairly definitively be traced to Wade Lyn, a Jamaican entrepreneur who arrived in Britain in the 1960's with his parents, and whose Hockley-based firm Island Delights is the biggest patty producer in the UK[xxiii].

Saveloys

Large, bright red coloured, sausages filled with finely-ground spiced pork. The name is possibly a variant of the French 'cervelat'. They're known in Britain at least since the 1790s[xxiv] from the firm of pork butchers Wall and Garland, of 33 Westgate St, Bath. Although they now turn up all over the place, they seem to be more-or-less a fixture in Southern Chip Shops.

In the Dickens' *Pickwick Papers* of 1837 we hear of "Mr. Solomon Pell ... regaling himself ... with a cold collation of an Abernethy biscuit and a saveloy."

Rag Pudding

Particularly associated with the town of Oldham. Minced meat, often including offal, folded into a very thin, rectangular, suet pastry and, most traditionally, steamed wrapped in a cloth rag. The pastry is very much thinner than usual in steamed puddings, hence the need for a rag, though modern commercial versions use a plastic film.

Hudibras by Samuel Butler is a long mock-epic poem, published in 1662 after the English Civil War, in which he makes fun of the silly Puritans. We're not quite sure if he's praising Rag Pudding or not with these lines...

> The high-shoe lords of Cromwell's making
> Were not for dainties, wasting, baking;
> The chiefest food they found most good in
> Was rusty bacon and rag pudding

Haggis

Haggis, the minced innards of a beast mixed with oatmeal and spices is nicely described in the great French cooking compendium *Larousse Gastronomique,* "Although its description is not immediately appealing, haggis has an excellent nutty texture and delicious savoury flavour". Which it has. Although we cannot doubt that haggis is now definitively Scottish and a staple of Scotland's Fish and Chip Shops, the first reference to the name is from a very curious old Lancashire cookery book from about 1430 known as the *Liber Cure Cocorum,* written in verse...

> **For hagese.**
> the hert of schepe, the nere thou take,
> tho bowel nowt thou shalle forsake,
> On the turbilen made, and boyled wele,
> Hacke alle togeder with gode persole,
> Isop, saveray, thou schalle take then,
> And suet of schepe take in, I ken,...

Older cookbooks, right up to the vast Victorian cookery reference book, *Cassell's* of 1888, distinguish between English Haggis, which adds bacon to minced sheep insides together with breadcrumb and strong flavourings, and Scottish Haggis which uses beef suet as the fat and oatmeal as the binder with more spicy flavourings of pepper and nutmeg.

All the same, the first reference in a book doesn't by any means say that it is the origin, as we've found repeatedly, though there are still one or two haggis-makers in Lancashire, and a 'Lancashire Haggis Company' in Chorley.

Pea Fritters

Pea fritters are battered and deep-fried mushy peas. Tricky to make, the usual practice is to chill the pea-mush first so it becomes stiff, shaping it into round patty to be battered and fried.

They seem to have started life as a distinctly vegetarian dish and we know they were included in a dinner hosted by The Vegetarian Society in 1884[xxv]. Since then pea fritters have come to prominence during the rationing of two World Wars, and, now at least two chip-shop suppliers produce pea fritters commercially.

Pies

Pies, along with their cousins the suet pudding, could be a whole book, and ought to be. We'll just mention Wigan, whose inhabitants are known as 'pie-eaters', which hosts a pie festival and has an annual pie-eating contest. Wigan chip shops provide the 'Wigan Slappy' consisting of a small meat pie, or on Fridays a meat-free Lancastrian 'butter pie', served inside a sliced barm cake (a large, soft, bread bun). This dish really exists.

Wigan's alternative 'national dish', the 'Wigan Kebab', consisting of a selection of pies on a snooker cue, doesn't seem to possess any reality beyond stage comedians, though that hasn't stopped the Wigan Warriors rugby club occasionally using it as a logo.

The Very Surprising History of Fish and Chips

DIETARY DATA

The following information is kindly supplied by the National Federation of Fish Fryers following nutritional tests using samples produced at the NFFF Training School in Leeds.

6 oz. portion of fish with 10 oz. chips and 4 oz. Mushy Peas:

Portion	Calories	Fat (Grams)
Total Portion Average	1086	52.9
Per 100g Average	187	9.2

6 oz. portion of fish with 10oz. chips:

Portion	Calories	Fat (Grams)
Total Portion Average	998.8	52.3
Per 100g Average	212.7	11.1

Chips cut to 14 x 17 mm in palm fat.

PORTION OF CHIPS (oz)	Calories	Fat (Grams)
5oz	295	11.9
10oz	589	23.8
15oz	884	35.7
20oz	1177	47.5
25oz	1473	59.5

Summary: Portion size has a huge impact on total fat and calories.

Different sizes of fish (Icelandic FAS Cod), with the same batter.

FISH SIZE (oz)	Calories	Fat per 100g
4oz Cod	227	16.7
6oz Cod	240	17.3
10oz Cod	265	20.3

Summary: Bigger fish contain more fat and calories per 100g, meaning that an accurate result cannot be obtained by simply testing one size of fish then applying to other sizes (i.e. testing a 4 oz fish and then multiplying by 2 to get results for an 8 oz fish).

3 different thicknesses of chips, fried in palm fat.

CHIP SIZE (mm)	Calories	Fat per 100g
14 x 14	220	8.6
14 x 17	208	8.3
17 x 17	212	9.0
14 x 17 (blanched)	225	8.7

Summary: A chip cut to the size of 14 x 17mm proved to be the healthiest in term of having fewer calories and less fat.

The same fish and chips, in 3 different frying mediums.

FRYING MEDIUM		Calories	TOTAL FAT (Grams)	SATURATED FAT(Grams)
Rapeseed Oil	Per portion	972	47.1	4.2
	Per 100g	202	9.8	0.9
Beef Dripping	Per portion	1028	56.6	30.9
	Per 100g	216	11.9	6.5
Palm Fat	Per portion	997	53.3	26.3
	Per 100g	220	11.7	5.8

Summary: Palm Fat and Beef Dripping offer similar results, Rapeseed Oil proved to be lower in calories and fat and much lower in saturated fat.

Overall Summary: Fish and chips are less than 10% fat if properly cooked and an average sized portion is less than 1000 calories. Adding peas to the meal lowers fat and calories per 100 grams, but as peas contain approximately 100 calories per 100 grams, this increases the total calories consumed in the meal.

Rapeseed oil (in optimum condition) produces the healthiest product, but breaks down more easily than other frying mediums. It is, however, a reasonable view that the customer expectation of taste is more important. The size of portion is key to total calories and fat consumed.

Item	Energy (Kcal)	Total Sugars *Enzymic*	Fat	Satur-ates	Trans Fatty Acids	Fibre *Aoac* Total	Sodium (Na) g
FISH & CHIPS [RAPESEED OIL]	972	1.92	47.1	4.2	0.05	20.2	0.12
MUSHY PEAS	97	0.40	0.6	0.1	0.01	6.0	0.21
TOTAL PORTION [581g]	1,069	2.32	47.7	4.3	0.06	26.2	0.32
PER 100g	184	0.40	8.2	0.7	0.01	4.5	0.06
FISH & CHIPS [BEEF DRIPPING]	1,028	1.90	56.6	30.9	1.86	15.7	0.42
MUSHY PEAS	97	0.40	0.6	0.1	0.01	6.0	0.21
TOTAL PORTION [576g]	1,125	2.30	57.2	31.1	1.87	21.7	0.63
PER 100g	195	0.40	9.9	5.4	0.32	3.8	0.11
CHIPS 14MM x 17MM [PALM OIL]	589	1.13	23.8	11.9	0.03	7.9	0.05
6oz COD [PALM OIL]	408	0.68	29.4	14.5	0.02	0.9	0.32
MUSHY PEAS	97	0.40	0.6	0.1	0.01	6.0	0.21
TOTAL PORTION [553g]	1,012	2.21	53.8	26.4	0.06	14.8	0.58
PER 100g	183	0.40	9.7	4.8	0.01	2.7	0.10
CHIPS 14MM x 17MM [BLANCHED & P/O]	637	1.13	24.6	12.2	0.03	11.9	0.07
6oz COD [PALM OIL]	408	0.68	29.4	14.5	0.02	0.9	0.32
MUSHY PEAS [3oz]	97	0.40	0.6	0.1	0.01	6.0	0.21
TOTAL PORTION [553g]	1,142	2.21	54.6	26.7	0.06	18.7	0.60
PER 100g	206	0.40	9.9	4.8	0.01	3.4	0.11

Item	Energy (Kcal)	Total Sugars Enzymic	Fat	Satur-ates	Trans Fatty Acids	Fibre Aoac Total	Sodium (Na) g
4oz COD [PALM OIL] CHIPS 14MM x 17MM	257	0.45	18.9	9.3	0.01	0.6	0.28
[P/O] 6oz	354	0.68	14.3	7.1	0.02	4.8	0.03
MUSHY PEAS [3oz] TOTAL PORTION	97	0.40	0.6	0.1	0.01	6.0	0.21
[383g]	707	1.53	33.8	16.5	0.04	11.3	0.51
PER 100g	185	0.40	8.8	4.3	0.01	3.0	0.13
10oz COD [PALM OIL]	750	1.13	57.4	28.3	0.03	1.7	0.59
CHIPS 14MM x 17MM [P/O] [10oz/283g] MUSHY PEAS	589	1.13	23.8	11.9	0.03	7.9	0.05
[100g/3oz] TOTAL PORTION	97	0.40	0.6	0.1	0.01	6.0	0.21
[666g]	1,436	2.66	81.8	40.3	0.07	15.6	0.85
PER 100g	216	0.40	12.3	6.1	0.01	2.3	0.13
10oz COD [PALM OIL]	750	1.13	57.4	28.3	0.03	1.7	0.59
CHIPS 14MM x 17MM [P/O] [10oz/283g] MUSHY PEAS	589	1.13	23.8	11.9	0.03	7.9	0.05
[7oz/198g] TOTAL PORTION	192	0.79	1.2	0.2	0.02	11.9	0.41
[764g]	1,531	3.06	82.4	40.4	0.08	21.5	1.05
PER 100g	200	0.40	10.8	5.3	0.01	2.8	0.14
TOTAL PORTION AVERAGE	1,146	2.33	58.8	26.5	0.32	18.6	0.65
PER 100g AVERAGE	196	0.40	9.9	4.5	0.05	3.2	0.11

ACKNOWLEDGEMENTS

The appearance of erudition in this book is largely thanks to the assistance of the National Federation of Fish Friers **nfff.co.uk**

and...

Project Gutenberg is a library of over 60,000 free eBooks all edited and maintained by volunteers **gutenberg.org**

The Internet Archive keeps a record of the entire internet and provides access to thousands of out-of-print books together with the ability to lend current books online, just as if you were at a real library **archive.org**

The British Newspaper Archive provides online access to some 58 million pages of British and Irish newspapers from the 1600s to today **britishnewspaperarchive.co.uk**

Frank Clement-Lorford devoted three years to intensive research into the life and career of Alexis Soyer at **alexis-soyer.com**

Pierre Leclerc has magnificently investigated the origin of potato chips in his website *La fabuleuse histoire de la pomme de terre frite* at **histoiredelafrite.com**

BIBLIOGRAPHY

History of Fish & Chips & the British Working Class 1870-1940, John K. Walton, 1992

The Jews and medicine, Harry Friedenwald, 1967

De Ratione Victus, Manuel Brudo, 1544

EU Fish Consumption, European Commission, 2020

The History And Social Influence Of The Potato, Redcliffe Salaman, 1949

Hunting The Hun, Captain James Belton and Lieutenant E. G. Odell, 1918

Two Men: A Romance of Sussex, Alfred Ollivant, 1910?

The Fish-Retailer and his Trade, Walter Wood, 1933

La fabuleuse histoire de la pomme de terre frite, Pierre Leclercq

Relish : the extraordinary life of Alexis Soyer, Victorian celebrity chef, Cowen, Ruth, 2006

Modern cookery for Private Families, Eliza Acton, 1845

A Shilling Cookery for The People, Alexis Soyer, 1845

The Art of Cookery, Made Plain and Easy, Hannah Glasse, 1747

Younger readers may like...

The Fabulous Tale of Fish and Chips, Helaine Becker, Illustrated by Omer Hoffman, 2010

REFERENCES

i   'On the Mode of Communication of Cholera', John Snow, 1849

ii   'Fish and chips and the British working class, 1870-1940', Walton, John K, 1992, p96

iii   Sheffield Evening Telegraph - Friday 20 February 1891, p2

iv   'The Forme of Cury - rolls of the Master-Cooks of King Richard II', transcribed by Samual Pegge, 1780

v   Roscommon Messenger - Saturday 23 September 1865, p2

vi   'Feast and Famine: Food and Nutrition in Ireland 1500-1920' L.A. Clarkson, E. Margaret Crawford, 2001

vii   'Regional differences in the mid-Victorian diet and their impact on health', Peter Greaves, 2000?

viii   Ministry of Agriculture and Fisheries, Report on the marketing of potatoes in England and Wales, 1926

ix   'Bolton Journal' 26 Sept 1924, referenced in Walton 1992 from Peter Taylor

x   Improvements Relating to Refrigerating Apparatus', A Einstein & AL Szilárd, U.S. Patent 178154111, 1930

xi   'British Newspapers: A History and Guide', Lake, Brian, 1984, p.213

xii   Newry Reporter - Saturday 04 December 1869, p4

xiii   Dundee Advertiser - Saturday 31 October 1891, p8

xiv   Dundee Courier - Tuesday 28 February 1882, p4

xv   Herald of Wales - Saturday 30 June 1888, p8

xvi   South Wales Daily News - Saturday 05 November 1887, p4

xvii   Newcastle Daily Chronicle - Tuesday 29 September 1891, p7

xviii   'Pattie Slappers: Stories from the Golden Age of Hull's Food Processing Industry', Nick Triplow, 2013 xix 'Deep and crisp and eaten: Scotland's deep-fried Mars bar', David S Morrison & Mark Petticrew, The Lancet 2004

xx 'A randomised crossover trial of the acute effects of a deep-fried Mars bar or porridge on the cerebral vasculature', William G Dunn, 2014

xxi Manchester Evening News - Saturday 10 December 1904 , p4

xxii Liverpool Echo - Tuesday 10 February 1914

xxiii Birmingham Mail – 16 September 2020

xxiv Bath Chronicle and Weekly Gazette - Thursday 17 October 1793

xxv Labour Leader - Friday 17 May 1912, p10

Printed in Great Britain
by Amazon

10577964R00061